IAN –

THANKS FOR ALL OF
YOUR ENCOURAGEMENT &
INSPIRATION –

YOU ARE SUCH A
BLESSING TO ME!

What others are saying about John...

"I met John in 2005 at one of my first HalfTime Institutes and our friendship began. I remember how he cast a vision of his heartfelt desire to help Christians identify and remove the barriers of money that exists between them and God. He is a student of his passion and it has been my joy to watch him grow in his knowledge and wisdom of God's word as he has pursued his calling. He is a visionary and has a special insight into the future of our Christian culture. John's an expert communicator, whether he is talking intimately with one person, speaking at a conference, or talking to thousands over radio or television. From the first time I met him, it was obvious that God had a special plan for the life of my friend John Putnam and God has uniquely equipped him to speak to this generation with his spiritually rich message of financial stewardship. He wants to change the world and I believe he can do it."

— **Bob Buford**, author of *HalfTime*,
Founder of Leadership Network

"John Putnam is passionate about helping transforming the perspectives others have on stewardship (or the lack thereof). He has counseled and helped countless people line up their financial priorities with what God's Word has to say. His radio feature, confident voice, his communication style and the colorful illustrations he uses brings scripture and stewardship principles to life. I'm convinced John has a voice that needs to be heard by as many people as possible."

— **Joe Paulo**, K-LOVE Director of Pledge Drives and Donor
Communication and former Director of Broadcasting,
New Life 91.9 WRCM & 89.7 WMHK

"Wise management of money is learned on the anvil of real life. John has lived out how to use money as a Kingdom tool leveraging it into blessing in his own family and advising thousands of other families. His convergence of wisdom, experience and world class communication skills, combines into this book and its surrounding tools. I believe John is the Ron Blue of our generation."

— **Lloyd Reeb**, author of *Success to Significance*,
international spokesman for HalfTime

"We are members of the John Putnam fan club. God is using his training, business success, and personal testimony to help others gain a God-focused understanding of stewardship and finances. We are grateful for his friendship and great counsel over the years!"

— **The Kendrick Brothers** (Alex & Stephen Kendrick), movie
producers of *War Room*, *Facing the Giants*, and *Fireproof*

"John Putnam's timeless financial wisdom, business advice, and organizational genius has greatly helped our rise to success as entrepreneurs. He is a tremendous asset to us professionally and personally, and this book contains much of what he's poured into our lives. You absolutely must read it, know it, and pass it on!"

— **David and Jason Benham**, real estate entrepreneurs and
authors of *Whatever the Cost*

"I've known and watched my good friend John Putnam over many years as he has ministered to couples regarding their finances. He is filled with uncommon wisdom and passion to see God's resources used for God's purposes. He is a gifted communicator and I know that this book will influence families in their financial decision-making, bring them closer to each other, and closer to Christ."

— **Ron Blue**, speaker,
author of *Master Your Money* and *Splitting Heirs*

"In He Spends She Spends, John shares creative and helpful ways to think about the 'why' of making money choices as we steward all that God has entrusted into our care. The practical steps he outlines in Chapter 9 alone are worth the read! If you will apply John's counsel found in this book, you will see the barriers that money can cause begin to diminish in your life and in your marriage and you will experience the joy that comes from being a wise steward."

— **David Wills**, President of National Christian Foundation

"John Putnam has done a masterful job in *He Spends She Spends* communicating why individuals and married couples will benefit from practicing God's way of handling money. Most impressive, John and his wife Anne have been living what they are teaching in this creative and helpful book. It is practical. It is biblical. It is life changing. I heartily recommend it."

— **Howard Dayton**, Founder of Compass

HE SPENDS
She Spends

HE SPENDS
She Spends

Why God Wants You To Live For Free

JOHN H. PUTNAM

Fedd Books
P.O. Box 341973
Austin, TX 78734
www.thefeddagency.com

Published in association with The Fedd Agency, Inc., a literary agency.
Unless otherwise indicated, Scripture quotations are taken from the *Holy Bible, New International Version*®, NIV®. Copyright © 1973, 1978, 1984, 2011 by Biblica, Inc.™ Used by permission of Zondervan. All rights reserved worldwide. www.zondervan.com. The "NIV" and "New International Version" are trademarks registered in the United States Patent and Trademark Office by Biblica, Inc.

Scripture quotations marked [NLT] are taken from the *Holy Bible*, New Living Translation, copyright ©1996, 2004, 2007, 2013 by Tyndale House Foundation. Used by permission of Tyndale House Publishers, Inc., Carol Stream, Illinois 60188. All rights reserved.

Scripture quotations marked [KJV] are from T*he Authorized (King James) Version*. Rights in the Authorized Version in the United Kingdom are vested in the Crown. Reproduced by permission of the Crown's patentee, Cambridge University Press.

ISBN: 978-1-943217-12-0
eISBN: 978-1-943217-15-1
Cover and Interior Design by: Lauren Hall
Printed in the United States of America
First Edition 15 14 13 10 09 / 10 9 8 7 6 5 4 3 2 1

Dedicated to my priceless family—
Anne, Jay, Lynn & Haley.
When we're together, that's home.

contents

please read this first...

There are a few things I'd like you to know. I'm just a guy who has been around people, their money, and their faith, and learned a lot. I've been making notes for this book for over a decade but God in his perfect timing recently opened up the door with authors, coaches, encouragers, and friends who helped make this a reality. My prayer is that this book would start a conversation, provide some fresh language, and give you a resource for thinking about and taking action on your money and financial choices from God's perspective. I wrote this in a casual style, as if you and I were just sitting on a porch somewhere talking about life.

This is a book about money that doesn't talk too much about actual dollars and cents. There are enough money books about money. You may have even been through a study of what the Bible says about money with Crown or Compass or worked through the practical side of money as you find in Ron Blue's *Master Your Money* or *Financial Peace University* by Dave Ramsey. That's great news. And if you haven't gone through those yet, let me highly recommend them to you and your small group. They offer some of the best training you can get. As a matter of fact, I believe this book will even be more helpful when used in conjunction with those excellent teachings.

I wrote my book because after seeing so many books about God and money, I realized there's still a gap. You may know what the Bible says about money and you may understand how to handle your money in a practical fashion, but I have found that many Christian families still have financial situations that are barriers between them and God's plans for their lives. I'm far from a theologian, but I believe it's because they may not understand why they make the choices they do and the spiritual factors that contribute to their choices.

That's what I pray that this book brings to the light. Think of this as a "why to" book rather than a "how to" book. After witnessing, and personally making, more financial mistakes than most people will ever individually experience, I want to share what I've learned through my own my walk with Christ, my personal financial journey and what I've observed from working with families and individuals like you for over twenty years as a financial advisor.

I want to take you into the motives, the messages, and the moments of your choices. I want us to explore the 90% of your financial iceberg that rests beneath the water that is rarely observed. I want to introduce you to your silent partners that automatically shape and influence your financial choices. We'll talk about stewardship, a "sleepy" word these days, but I want to bring it to life. I'll share new insights and walk you through fresh practical steps to bring clarity and unity to your plans.

Most of all, I want to help you remove money as a barrier between you and your relationship with Jesus. To bring you closer to Christ and away from the influences around your money. I want you to flourish without your finances dragging you down and to see money as a tool that can glorify God, not as a goal that can take you away from Him.

If we aim our hearts, our lives, and our resources at the Father, it might just give us the best chance to live like heaven right here on earth and find freedom in Christ rather than in our money.

Welcome to *He Spends, She Spends: Why God Wants You to Live for Free.*

A FEW NOTES ABOUT THE FORMAT

- When you get to the end of each chapter you will find a section called *Reflection* that I hope will enhance your reading experience

- *Change for your Dollar* summarizes key messages

- *Money in Motion* poses questions for consideration and action

- *Prayer* places this all in the proper perspective

- Additional downloadable resources, videos, etc. are on my website at www.JohnHPutnam.com

it's not about the money

So God created mankind in His own image, in the image of God He created them; male and female He created them.

—Genesis 1:27

The room lit up in a soft glow as I pushed the power button of my cell phone . . . 3:14 a.m.

Lord, please not again tonight. John, just go back to sleep, I tell myself.

But I can't. My mind races with regret.

I should've made better choices when I had the chance. How have I let this happen? What about the future? College for our kids? Lord, please forgive me . . . again.

My mind was spinning, I of all people should know better, for goodness sake. I'm supposed to help others manage their resources, and look at me. If others only knew the mistakes I've made with my own finances. I'm exhausted. I thought this Christian life was supposed to be easier by now. Lord, will you please help me get back to sleep, I need to rest.

But it was too late. My worry wake-up call was at full volume. The weight of our finances pressed on my mind like my fat cat Pepper, sleeping on my head. Regret from the past and fear of the future covered me like the blanket I was under. How did a 2 $5/8$ x 6 $1/8$ inch piece of green and white paper get this much power in my life?

Morning came too soon. I grabbed a cup of coffee and a shower and then got dressed. No time this morning to pause for reading the Bible and spending a few unrushed moments with God. I needed to get moving. Things usually look better in the light of day, and today that was true. Maybe that was God's way of saying it was okay that I skipped our time together. I would get caught up with Him

> *How did a 2⅝ x 6⅛ inch piece of green and white paper get this much power in my life?*

tomorrow. Too much to do right now. I needed to take action. I needed to fix this.

Of course I did, I'm a guy. Guys want to fix things. The weight of financial responsibility could be a really heavy burden, but I usually just wound up pushing that emotion down in my gut every time it came up. The pressure of that responsibility was like a helium balloon that kept rising. I knew I should share the burden with my wife, Anne, but I didn't. Yep. Once again, I'm a guy. It would be exhausting, but I was going to give it one more try.

I made some promises to myself: *I'm going to work harder. I'm going to work smarter. I'm going to get my arms around our finances and make plans to do better, to make better choices, to be the leader God made me to be.* I paused briefly to ask God for His blessings on my new action items, and then went to the kitchen to see Anne and the kids before heading to the office and getting to work.

As I stepped into the room, I got a hug and kiss from my bride of twenty-six years, and she presented me with something else. Why is there always something else?

"Honey, remember the trip we talked about?" she asked as she grabbed a handful of papers. "I just went through all these forms and instructions, and the first deposit is due today or she can't go on the trip. It's $300. What do you want to do?"

A few months earlier we had a brief conversation about a school trip for one of our kids. It looked like a great opportunity so we quickly agreed to sign her up. We didn't talk much about it at the time, nor had we since. Now that we had to make a quick decision, I marveled at how quickly my attitude changed. I was about to go from hero to zero in the time it took to answer my wife.

"Why are we just now talking about this on the day that it is due?" I responded less than calmly. "Why can't you help us stay on top of these things? We've talked about you getting more involved with the family finances but it never happens!"

As soon as the words left my lips I wished I could take them back. That helium-filled balloon of financial responsibility rose up once again at the absolute wrong time. Definitely not my best moment.

When we decided our child could take this trip, we felt we could swing the added expense. We didn't pray about it or ask anyone's opinion about it, and I hadn't thought about it since. I was unprepared and embarrassed. So, of course, instead of admitting that and leaning into this decision together, I mentally rehearsed all the reasons this was *her* fault. Why was she always looking to me for all the answers? Why was she deferring to me? Couldn't she take a little responsibility once in a while?

This was a perfect example of a *money moment*—a real life situation involving our money, with motives and messages affecting our choices, resulting in real consequences. However, this episode was not just about money. It went deeper. It's what I call a money mirage—an issue that appears to be financial, but it is something much more elusive and complex. We were like so many couples. The money mirage often hides what's really going on underneath—unknown, unobserved, untouched.

> *The money mirage often hides what's really going on underneath—unknown, unobserved, untouched.*

"Send the money," I snapped in a tone that was as cold as ice. "I'll transfer some funds," I grumbled as I started thumbing the numbers into my cell phone. The obligatory, "I love you," rolled off of my frustrated lips and I slammed the door as an exclamation point.

Off I went—the self-proclaimed godly man and leader of the Putnam household. I reminded myself to omit this little episode from my "Husband of the Year" application. Another maddening money moment had come and gone. It looked nothing like the life I am trying to lead. I'm pretty sure you know what I'm talking about.

I love God and want to follow Christ's teaching, but I don't always seem to measure up, especially when it comes to money. There never seemed to be enough because of the many competing priorities—and they seemed to be expanding. I wanted to be a good provider for our family. Anne wanted to feel secure. My kids wanted to "fit in" and have the things their friends had. We wanted to give them fun experiences to help them learn and grow. And what about college? These money moments kept showing up in our lives at every turn and seemed to be involved in everything we were doing. How did this happen? Something had changed since we were starting out together. I was earning more money but I was enjoying it less and worrying about it more. I thought that by the time I got to this point in my life, this would be easier.

A DANGEROUS DUO

As I headed off to work, I was immediately overcome with regret. That was no way to talk to the woman I love. We're a team— she lets me be the leader, and I accept that role. I wouldn't be who I am and I couldn't do what I do without her. So I called Anne and apologized

Me and my money— we're a dangerous duo

for my bad behavior, and she, as usual, was gracious. She's had plenty of practice after dealing with me for so many years.

But, why did it always take an argument or a problem for me to stop and think more reasonably about these issues that kept coming up? Years ago I said yes to Jesus, and I have been trying to follow Him and enjoy the abundant life He promised, yet little had changed in the way I handled my own financial decisions. Me and my money—we're a dangerous duo. Sound familiar?

Jesus promised that He would make me a new person if I surrendered everything to Him. I know a great gift when I see one, and I needed His, so I said yes. I told Him I would follow Him. I wanted to obey Him and trust Him. And I meant it. I just forgot to tell my money.

I've been a trusted financial advisor for many years, helping people make wise decisions about money, even though my own record was a little challenging. As an advisor, I can talk with a couple, look at their situation on paper, and know exactly what they need to do, how it should be done, and how best to encourage them toward success. But, when it comes to me and my financial goals and objectives, I've got serious blind spots, as we all do.

Confession is always a good place for me to start, and for you as well. I can see a family's financial situation from a mile away, but can remain blind and entrapped in my own. I know I'm not the only Christian who's been fooled by a money mirage. During my professional career, which spans more than twenty-five years, I've advised in over 15,000 conversations with individuals and families like yours, and guess what . . . in almost every conversation, a money mirage hovers like an unwelcome guest.

Our respective financial issues may be as distinct as our fingerprints, but we have at least one thing in common: our money problems are not solely about money. As I unpack this more, you will see that the elephant in the room is very real, very large, and very heavy. There is more going on in and around your financial choices than you ever imagined. Yet we continually try to convince ourselves that our money problems are totally about money. This usually shows up in seemingly powerful statements containing a little bitty word that packs a really big punch: IF. "If I could just get a little bit ahead in the race . . . ," "If I get that raise . . .

> *There is more going on in and around your financial choices than you ever imagined.*

," "If we had a bigger house . . . ," "If we just had more money . . . ", "If we could join that club . . ." I've seen it time and time again with couples, our partnership with money creates a dangerous duo, creating confusion, changing perspectives, sapping our energy, distracting us from what is most important and often driving a wedge between us and those we love the most. Allow me to uncover a well-kept secret of money moments. It's not about the money.

Does this sound familiar? You may have had a recent conversation that is eerily similar to mine and Anne's. Don't feel alone; we all do it. The "IF" game takes us to a place in the future that always seems to feel better than where we are now. This can't possibly be the way God intended for us handle our finances.

Interestingly, for something that can cause so much mayhem, money is a relatively simple tool. When you put *money in motion*, you can really only do two things with it: you can *consume* it,

> *There's a place where math stops and you begin.*

or you can *share* it. When you consume it, you can *spend* it today, you can *save* it and spend it soon, or, you can *invest* it and hopefully spend it (or give it away) in the future. When you share it, you can *give* it to those in need, or you can share it as you pay your *taxes*. And finally, to oversee your money well, you need to *plan* and you need wise *counsel*. But when you put these seven items together in the context of life, it doesn't feel too simple.

Let me share an insight that I realized many years ago. There's a place where math stops and you begin. This was that place for us. The argument we had wasn't about sending the money or balancing our online accounts—that's simple arithmetic. Ultimately it was about me; past choices dealing with who I trusted with "my" money. God or me?

There are few topics in the Bible that God spends as much time on as He does with the topic of money, wealth, and possessions. There are more than 2,300 verses in the Bible and I've seen them all. You may wonder, *why so many?* I believe it's because God understood the power of money to draw us away from complete dependence on Him. Now please don't misunderstand me. You can

> You can have God and you can have money, but you <u>cannot</u> love them both.

have God and you can have money, but you <u>cannot</u> love them both. If we try, that's when our desires and emotions cause the conflicts and burdens that create the toxic nature that surrounds money. Or as the Bible puts it:

> *For the love of money is a root of all kinds of evil.*
> *Some people, eager for money,*
> *have wandered from the faith and pierced*
> *themselves with many griefs.*
> —1 Timothy 6:10

I think one of the reasons God may have given us money is so we could also use it to get a quick look into what is important to us. Think of your money in motion like a financial Instagram—it's quick, it's to the point, and it communicates exactly what is happening at that moment. If you were to show me your Mint.com weekly summary, I could tell you pretty accurately where your heart is headed. These choices reveal things about us—our priorities and what we believe.

Most families make money decisions with a dangerous blindness to the forces that impact those decisions. For example, why did you have to have that particular new car or live in that particular neighborhood? Unfortunately, the impact of society, social media, and the opinions of those around us don't end in middle school. From the outside, we look "healthy, wealthy, and wise," navigating our respective journeys with skill and knowledge, becoming successful, and growing. Yet on the inside, many of us are dealing with concerns that run counter to our Christian faith and make us feel more like we are *broken, poor, and imprisoned.*

> *Most families make money decisions with a dangerous blindness to the forces that impact those decisions.*

From my thousands of conversations with couples—as well as from my own experiences—here's how most of us relate to money. We are:

- frozen by fears,
- burdened by regrets,
- distracted by beliefs,
- derailed by behaviors, and
- challenged by perspective.

And this results in:

- thinking more about money than God,
- wanting more than we have,
- holding on to the past,
- looking for our security from our money, and
- making "me first" choices.

It's no wonder Anne and I avoided talking about the trip deposit until the last minute. We can talk about anything under the sun; but, when money comes up, we experience the not-so-humorous "failure to communicate." It doesn't matter who did the spending; when it comes to talking about money, we're spent. Why? Why is it so difficult to discuss something so important with the most important person in your life? For starters, it has a lot to do with each of our unique experiences with money and what happens when our experiences crash into each other.

> *It doesn't matter who did the spending; when it comes to talking about money, we're spent.*

When most of us started our careers, we joined a journey already in progress that normalized the feelings and convictions I just listed. In other words, this was just the way money matters were "spozed" to be. When we were looking for that first job, many of us "sold ourselves" to the highest bidder with little concern or awareness of how that decision may have complemented or detracted from God's plans and His work in our lives. Or, more likely, we told ourselves that God provided us with a great job, so we signed on the dotted line, read our new job description, and the company enrolled us in their training program so they could begin to shape us into who they needed us to be.

Before we knew it, reality hit us like a freight train—business goals, benefits, and retirement plans, then, houses, babies, and college funds, and somewhere in the mix a new kitchen or deck awaits! Life took off following directions on a map drawn by someone else. Was God in front or behind us? We lost track of Him.

The farther we went up this ladder, the farther we had to fall.

> *Comparison destroys contentment, then creates it.*

We became distant from our truest self, closer to the world, and the way home got cloudier and murkier as we joined so many others along this well-worn highway.

Back in the day, it would have bugged you to look and act like everyone else. But now, for some reason it offers a strange sense of comfort. Comparison destroys contentment, then creates it. You will find plenty of Christians just like you at every socio-economic level you experience. It's easy then for comparison to make you feel at ease. If everyone else is okay with this, why should I be worried? This spiral can go on for years and years. Unfortunately, many of us continue stumbling along until we get the gold watch . . . or worse.

Some get a strategic interruption. Something happens that shocks them, brings them immediately into the present. Most of these interruptions are unpleasant—a serious health scare, the death of a loved one, a job layoff. After the shock wears off, a refreshing clarity appears if we remember that God's actions all lead to good results. God often has ways to "interrupt" our plans and refocus our attention on Him. He has laid an opportunity in front of you to find Him once again.

> God often has ways to "interrupt" our plans and refocus our attention on Him.

Are you stumbling forward, unaware? If that's the case, it might take an event like that to bring you to your senses. But, there's another, better option to clearing away the haze of the mirage. Remember back in elementary school when the crossing guards taught you how to safely cross a street? Stop, look, and listen. This is exactly what we will do together in this book. But for so many of us our money moments turn into mayhem. We have bought so deeply into the world's view of money and success that it can appear far too difficult to change and far too painful to dismantle things. As we work together, you will retrace your steps, find your original path again, start over, and begin to rebuild. So together, we will stop and take a deep breath, look to God's word, and listen for His still, small voice that speaks peace. It is a friendly voice, because God has always been for you, not against you.

As you listen and focus your attention on Him, the volume of

His voice will begin to grow. Clear and true answers flow from his voice in response to your heartfelt queries. *Has this voice been there all along?* you ponder. *How have I missed it all these years?* As we look to God's word, a renewed peace and faith will begin to slowly seep in like a drink of cool water on a hot, hazy day. As the haze begins to clear, a new journey will come into focus, but there is work yet to do.

Most of us know what we need to do, and even how to do it. By looking at the "why to" we will get to the heart of our money mayhem. I want it to peel back the onion one layer at a time until we get to the core of the matter.

Hear me, friend, when I say this. It's not that I have all of the answers. However, I have made or seen most every financial mistake you can make and lived to tell about it. Now I have a passion and a calling to share what I've learned. To let you into some of what I've experienced personally or seen through others so you have the greatest chance to become what God intended without money getting in the way. I hope to refresh the language around our financial issues. I won't be showing you how to balance your checkbook or which investment tool to

> *The world's better never quite measures up to God's best.*

use, but I pray to help you understand the complexities around your financial choices. I want to expose our "silent partners" that guide those choices. Then, give you answers for why we so often find ourselves dealing with worry and want around money when our Lord has cautioned us about material things like our clothes, our homes, our food (see Matthew 6:25).

As we begin this new journey together, you will find that there is much between you and your destination. Most of it you believed, you built, or you bought. You may have to give up images of your old life. You may be ridiculed by others. You definitely will be questioned by your friends—even your friends from church—and your colleagues at work. They might think you're nuts. And why not? They probably can't even fathom what God

> *Prayer and action are God's one-two punch.*

is doing in their own lives. The world's better never quite measures up to God's best. But take heart. We begin this new journey with an old promise: "I am with you always. . . . " What better companion is there to guide you back to an exciting and fulfilling adventure waiting to be discovered?

Remember: "My money and me" is a dangerous duo. Your old thinking and old actions have gotten you to where you are. To get to where God wants you to go will require a new perspective and new actions. Prayer and action are God's one-two punch. Or as James puts it, "...faith and deeds...". That's sounds like true stewardship.

> *In the same way, faith by itself, if it is not accompanied by action, is dead.*
> —James 2:17

The term stewardship gets used a lot in church, and Bible studies, and Christian conversations. I hear it referred to often as our "time, talents, and treasure." Yes, that's a part of stewardship, but that statement leaves so much unsaid and does not come close to capturing the depth of what God had in mind. Let me put it even simpler. Stewardship is every choice you make after you say "yes" to Jesus. Every choice. Every moment. Every resource. Every purchase.

> *Stewardship is every choice you make after you say "yes" to Jesus.*

Every breath held captive for Him and Him alone. Just as Bach signed his letters, "SDG"—Soli Deo Gloria —"To God alone be the glory." Stay tuned . . . we're going to dig into this a lot more later.

So, what does "prayer and action" look like around our financial stewardship? For starters, maybe we can learn a lesson from my teenaged self.

I have always liked watching sports mainly for one reason. It gives me a good backdrop to have a break and maybe take a nap. I learned that one from my dad. I'm one of five boys, and we grew up on a Black Angus cattle farm. Dad traveled most days of the week, so when Saturday rolled around it was time to get work done. Hard work. We built gates and fences, loaded hay, cut wood, helped around the house; you get the picture. One thing was for sure. Dad loved working on the farm after his week at his "real job," and taking a Saturday afternoon off was unheard of— at least until as a teenager I partially cracked the code.

It turns out that my Dad loved to watch golf and any ball game from his alma mater, the UNC Tar Heels; these were some of the only things he would allow to distract him from work on the farm. So during golf and ball seasons, before we would head out to work the farm on Saturday mornings, I would scour the papers for any of these sports and then casually drop it into our morning conversation at just the right time. Genius. Every now and then, my simple strategy worked and I found myself on the couch on a Saturday, playing cards, watching a ballgame while my Dad napped between plays. It was perfect. There was work to be done, but I found myself resting with my father.

Old model: farm work on a Saturday. New perspective, new action: a nap and cards on the couch. Okay, maybe that's not really biblical, but you get the point—new perspective followed by new action can change your current situation.

Moses demonstrated prayer and action when many of the Israelites became ill while roaming the desert in search of the Promised Land. With limited medical expertise it did not look promising for the sick. Through prayer and God's direction, Moses was obedient when he wrapped a snake around a long pole and held it up in the desert. All who looked upon the snake were healed. Interestingly, if you look at the logo of the American Medical Association, it remains a representation of this pole that Moses held up in the desert. Little did Moses know that lifting the snake would be symbolic of the day when the Son of Man would be lifted up and heal more than just an illness.

Just as Moses lifted up the snake in the wilderness,
so the Son of Man must be lifted up.
—John 3:14

New perspective, new action. These words of Jesus capture the essence of stewardship. The new life that we have been given was made possible by Christ's sacrifice on the cross, and all that we do—including the way we manage our money—must lift Christ up. When our financial decisions honor Christ, we will then achieve true riches. Our choices will be clear and true and we will be immune to the destructive nature of the dangerous duo as we focus on the Savior instead of the world. Every financial choice becomes holy in the shadow of the cross.

> *Every financial choice becomes holy in the shadow of the cross.*

Anne and I still have our tough "money moments," and so will you. They are unavoidable. But now that we have a clearer understanding of what rests beneath those choices and how God wants us to depend completely on Him, those moments rarely include doors slamming or harsh words. (We may be getting better, but we're not perfect!) Remember: it's a journey; but the ride will be a lot more fun than it has been, and along the way you will learn that you really can trust God to take care of you.

He wants to do the same for you. So let's begin a new adventure—one that will free you from your money worries by giving you an abundance of true riches. I can think of no better place to start than "In the beginning"—that brief yet blissful arrival at your own little Garden of Eden.

REFLECTION

CHANGE FOR YOUR DOLLAR

1) Most money concerns have little to do with actual dollars and cents.
2) When the team consists of only you and money, it becomes a dangerous duo.
3) We form expectations around money that are not rooted in God's perspective and therefore do not support His plans for us.
4) Changing your perspective and taking new action will change your situation.
5) Honoring Christ in your financial decisions yields true riches.

MONEY IN MOTION

1) Think of a common financial disagreement in your home and ask yourself if it really is about money. If not, consider what might be behind the conflict.
2) Describe a recent "worry wake-up call" and think about what financial concerns were involved.
3) If you know someone who has experienced a "strategic interruption," think about the outcome and whether it ultimately was a positive result.
4) You might think having more money would make your life easier. If your situation were to stay the same and you didn't get more money, think of three actions you could take to ease your financial pressures.

PRAYER

I've often let my mind, heart, and actions be overtaken by financial concerns instead of overtaken by my love for you. You mercifully offer peace in the midst of our busy lives that can only be found in you. Help me to rest in the simplicity and wealth of you and you alone. Amen.

starting together

God blessed them and said to them, "Be fruitful and increase in number; fill the earth and subdue it. Rule over the fish in the sea and the birds in the sky and over every living creature that moves on the ground." Then God said, "I give you every seed-bearing plant on the face of the whole earth and every tree that has fruit with seed in it. They will be yours for food." God saw all that He had made, and it was very good.

—Genesis 1:28-29, 31

Most couples have a "remember when" story. It normally starts with a grin and it usually goes something like this:

"Remember our first apartment? It seemed like we were always eating tuna casserole or tuna salad on toast; but, at the time, it was as good as steak and potatoes."

Or . . .

"We didn't have any furniture so we just put our mattress on the floor. It was so much fun—like camping out every night."

Or . . .

"We only had one car starting off, but the carpools and conversations with my co-workers never failed to be a great way to get a work day off the ground!"

Or . . .

"We couldn't afford ornaments for our first Christmas tree, but she had saved all the ribbons from our wedding presents and attached them to our little tree--that was easily the best Christmas I remember."

Every couple has one of these stories about how they scraped by and found joy in every bit of life during that time because love covered every moment and money was not yet a distraction.

For Anne and me, it was our big brown sectional couch— yards of a brown cloth that was so indestructible and stain resistant that it had to have been developed by NASA! I say "our," but in reality we didn't really own it at first. It was on loan from my brother who hauled it over to our place and told us we could buy it from him in installments. That big old beast of a couch didn't match a thing in our house, but we didn't mind. (Okay, full disclosure, Anne minded, but understood. She's awesome that way.) It was clean, comfortable, and made our otherwise barren family room look like, well . . . a family room. We felt like the king and queen of our 1800 square foot palace. That misfit couch became a part of our household along with the outdoor folding table that served as our kitchen table, along with the odd assortment of chairs and dressers that somehow found their way into our home from family and friends. Today, designers would call it "eclectic." (We were ahead of our time.)

That couch was what I remember most, though I almost hate to mention it because I think I still owe my brother $1,100. Actually, after never being able to make the installments, we pretty much gave up and my brother graciously said, "It's yours." Thanks Harry!

Our first bed was a wedding present from my parents. Actually it was a headboard and two dressers. We had no curtains or window treatments, and no money to buy them, so Anne's mom bought fabric and came to our cozy little house in Charlotte, measured the windows, and made the

> *Early on in most relationships, either the man or the woman begins to put pressure on the other to go bigger and better.*

curtains for us. Then she made pillows for the brown sectional in the family room. We would have been fine without the curtains or the pillows, but our parents wanted to help us, and we were more than grateful for their support. What a blessing. It all made our little place look so classy.

To us, almost everything was an upgrade. We met in college, and neither of us had much money. We couldn't afford to go out to eat, so for our "dates," we would go to the grocery store and buy a loaf of bread, a bag of Cheetos, a 2-liter bottle of soda, and a package of bologna. That was it! I have to admit it made me love Anne more. I have learned that early on in most relationships, either the man or the woman begins to put pressure on the other to go bigger and better. Not once did Anne make me feel like less of a boyfriend because I couldn't take her to a nice restaurant or buy her expensive gifts. If you're a guy reading this, you know how cool that is. So, when we recently celebrated the 30th anniversary of the day we met, guess what my dinner surprise was for Anne? You got it. A plate of bologna sandwiches, Cheetos, and a big old ice-cold bottle of soda! We had a laugh with our stroll down memory lane, and I'm pretty sure Anne made something else to eat that night. It turns out Anne doesn't really like bologna, but she loves me!

Our three children were born during the years we lived in that little house, and some of my best memories were from Saturday mornings. I was on early daddy duty and Anne got to sleep late. After a long workweek, the early mornings were painful, but time has a way of smoothing out the rough edges of a memory. It was a similar scene each Saturday morning. First stop, coffee pot. Next stop, pull out the large multi-colored cardboard blocks and the basket of "bullies" from the corner. The "bullies," named by my son, were different kinds of action figures that my parents had bought for ten to twenty-five cents each in the small town ministries shop where they volunteer. The little TV in the corner remained silent as the kids and I had playtime, building towers out of cardboard blocks as the sun streamed through the corner windows. Up the towers would go, adding the bullies on every level, then jumping through them to knock them down. Rebuild, repeat. There was no place I rather would have been. I had no desire for anything more than what we had. All was right with the world.

Now I'm smart enough to realize "the good old days" weren't always all that good. I'm sure there were times when we were getting close to the end of the month and the checking account was running dry, or days when my job wore me down. But our memories of starting together are great, and here's why: as newlyweds, being together was more important than having stuff. Or to put it another way, as long as we had each other, a roof over our heads, food to eat and a few things to sit on, sleep on, or eat on, life was really good.

> *...but I gave them this command: Obey me, and I will be your God and you will be my people. Walk in obedience to all I command you, that it may go well with you.*
> —Jeremiah 7:23

Starting out, we were all we had. Everything was new, and we genuinely wanted to please each other, honor each other. So recently and earnestly in love, sitting on that old couch and sharing what happened in our jobs that day wasn't something we did because a marriage counselor told us to. We did it because it was fun, and frankly, we couldn't afford to do much else most evenings. Of course, this was all after we watched the requisite "Disney Sing-a-Long" VHS tape with the kids! (For all those in their twenties reading this, VHS = DVD. Never mind, just go to Netflix.)

FRIENDS AND COMMUNITY

For entertainment, we might invite another couple over to play board games on that rickety kitchen table. There was no Xbox or

Wii Sports. They brought the drinks; we made popcorn. In fact, living in a neighborhood with a bunch of other couples in the same boat was all the entertainment we needed. It was effortless. We were building a community of friendships with couples like us.

We lived in a little cul-de-sac, and as I turned onto our street on Friday afternoons it was almost as if someone organized a street festival. Dads would be out throwing frisbee or tossing a ball to their kids. There would be Anne and the other moms, hanging out with the kids in someone's front yard. By the time I parked the car, ran into the house to change into something comfortable, people were coming out of their houses carrying stuff. Dishes. Coolers. Folding tables. Chairs. Before you knew it, parents and kids were lined up at a grill holding open an open bun as someone's dad dropped a sizzling dog onto it. I know this sounds crazy, but even the food seemed to taste better when all we could afford was the simple stuff.

> If you want to make a memory, just mix together simple, relational, and joyful.

Occasionally, someone would stop at the movie rental place (Remember those?) and bring home a comedy—VHS, of course. I remember one night we were watching *What About Bob* and the chicken-eating scene was so funny that we all pitched in and went to KFC to get a bucket of chicken. Anne and I still laugh thinking about that night when we were sprawled out in that living room eating fried chicken and watching that movie together. If you want to make a memory, just mix together simple, relational and joyful. It's a recipe that is sure to impress.

Shortly after we moved in to our house, it dawned on me that I now had a lawn to mow and bushes to trim. I had an older mower, but no trimmer; and it didn't matter. Inevitably, every Saturday, some of us got together and swapped tools. None of us could afford to have everything we needed. This exercise not only allowed us to get our chores done without buying a lot of stuff, it added to a wonderful sense of community. You didn't just go over to a guy's garage and take his lawn mower or his trimmer without asking. You'd knock on his door and he would come out with a cup of coffee. You'd likely visit a while talking about your kids, your marriage, your work—laughing together and getting caught up on neighborhood news. You almost forgot why you stopped by in the first place because standing around a garage drinking coffee with a friend on a Saturday morning was exactly what you needed.

Can you believe that all of this fun happened because you did not own every tool and gadget you "needed" to survive this journey called life? It forced us together and God had a way of looking out for us, even when we may not have been looking for Him.

You know those big front porches attached to everyone's enormous houses these days? Ever see anyone sitting on them? Drive through a nice development some evening and count the number of people sitting on their front porches. Our porches in that first neighborhood were not much more than what some people call stoops—a little concrete square at the top of the steps with room for maybe two folding chairs. But many evenings we'd sit out there on the steps and neighbors would walk by and stop and we'd talk for a while. Or we

> *Busy makes you plan.*
> *Stuff slows you down.*
> *Money can be an*
> *isolator.*

might be the ones taking a walk, stopping to talk to whoever else was sitting on their front porches because that's what you did when you didn't have a lot of money or stuff that needed your attention. Ironically, our lack of financial resources enabled us to enjoy the things that so many of us crave today. We were content. Something was better than nothing and nothing satisfied more than being together.

All the believers were together and had everything in common...

*They broke bread in their homes and ate
together with glad and sincere hearts.*
—Acts 2:44, 46

Busy makes you plan. Stuff slows you down. Money can be an isolator. These Friday and Saturday evening gatherings with neighbors were never really planned. They just sort of happened.

ENTER "THE WHISPER"

Now trust me—I know we all tend to romanticize the past. We tend to gloss over the messy stuff and forget the reality of our struggles. I cannot speak with any personal authority, but I have been told by my wife, that women forget the pain of childbirth, which probably explains why so many of us have more than one child. Similarly, our mind has a way to block out or downplay the hardships of those early years. There were tough times, but to be honest, we didn't really worry much about money or things. Did we want to someday to have more money? Of course. Regardless, the questions that swirl around money didn't keep us up at night. We had each other; we had friends; we had community; and that was enough. At least for a brief period, we had what felt like our own little Garden of Eden. It was as if we were listening to what God said to Adam and Eve: "Look, kids—I've made you. I've created this beautiful environment for you to live in. Enjoy. Everything you need, I will provide. So be satisfied."

Our little Eden paled in comparison to the garden God provided for Adam and Eve, but it was pretty nice. Actually, it was awesome. We had a warm house, warm food, and warm friends. And we had each other. What more could you ask for?

Just open your garage door and look in your closets. Do you realize that even during a recession, one of the fastest growing businesses in the U.S. has been the rental storage facility business? Our big houses and bigger garages aren't big enough for all the stuff we own, so we rent places to house it. And even when choosing to move to a smaller place or faced with having to downsize a home, we won't let go of our stuff, so we pay to store it.

What happened? When did we always get to be first in line? If we look to the world, we see this a lot. There's a reason for that. For starters, this is nothing new, as we see in the parable of the wealthy farmer:

> *And he told them this parable: "The ground of a certain rich man yielded an abundant harvest. He thought to himself, 'What shall I do? I have no place to store my crops.' "Then he said, 'This is what I'll do. I will tear down my barns and build bigger ones, and there I will store my surplus grain. And I'll say to myself, "You have plenty of grain laid up for many years. Take life easy; eat, drink and be merry."' "But God said to him, 'You fool! This very night your life will be demanded from you. Then who will get what you have prepared for yourself?' "This is how it will be with whoever stores up things for themselves but is not rich toward God."*
>
> —Luke 12:16-21

This guy was probably not a bad guy. He ran a farming business. He had a big harvest, needed somewhere to put it, and his first inclination was, "I'll keep it for myself. I deserve a break. I harvested it. It's mine." This may sound very familiar. How many times have you had a windfall, or extra "something" and your first thought is about you and your desires/ needs? It doesn't take much imagination to put yourself in this guy's shoes and come up with a similar response. I know I've done this. Whether then, or now, I know that God's response

We need to pay attention to God's plan for our resources in the midst of abundance and scarcity.

is the same. The farmer's answer? Build a bigger barn. God's answer? Not so fast. The takeaway? We need to pay attention to God's plans for our resources in the midst of abundance and scarcity. But there is often much more influencing our heads and our hearts.

For most of us it's complicated, but its roots can be traced back to a common origin and we must be willing to bring it into this conversation. You see, if it were just us and God, it would be a little clearer to spot the issue at hand. God's

> *Life's tough, but it's even tougher when you make poor decisions.*

perfect. I'm not. Problem solved. But there's another influence around us that doesn't want any of this to happen. Enter the whisper of an enemy. An enemy that works through his own plans of distraction and his own devices of destruction and they don't include you following God's plans of redemption.

Maybe I need to stop here and explain something. I realize people don't like talking about "the devil"—even church people. But I believe there's an enemy and I believe that this enemy's primary goal is to do whatever is necessary to capture our attention and our hearts away from God. Sometimes it can be by simply distracting us from God and His plans for us. But do not misunderstand, whether his methods are simple or complex, the enemy, this thief, wants to take it all.

The thief comes only to steal and kill and destroy...
—John 10:10a

At the same time, not all of our financial issues can be blamed on the enemy ("...the devil made me do it"—a quote not from scripture). A lot of times we just make poor choices for a variety of reasons. But poor choices just make the enemy's job easier. Let me put it more simply: Life's tough, but it's even tougher when you make poor decisions.

One thing I have learned over the years about the enemy is that he is patient and he is sometimes so very subtle. It's also been said that while "the enemy may be clever, he is not wise." I'm sure during those early years I saw the slick magazine ads and television commercials telling me I needed a nicer car, better clothes, a boat, a country-club membership. I didn't bite. At least not at first. From the enemy's perspective, that's okay. After he tempted Jesus in the wilderness, the Bible says the enemy "left him until an opportune time" (see Luke 4:13). He always waits patiently for the opportune time. For me it was lunch with a friend and one of his friends who tagged along. It turned out to be a very expensive lunch—one still impacting me after twenty plus years. More on that later.

Fast forward to three houses later, I reflect back on those wonderful early years together and realize that even with a memory that will smooth out the hardships, we had something the soul craves, something money cannot buy: Joy. We had contentment, friends concerned about each other—"doing life together." We knew our friends and our friends knew us.

A number of years ago, a client who owned a business asked me to help one of his employees with some financial planning. I was happy to do it—I really enjoy showing people how to manage their finances and prepare for the future—but the majority of my clients were, by the world's standards, wealthy, and this employee wasn't. Because of that, the only time he could meet with me was on a Saturday, but I didn't work weekends.

So, when I got in my car on the appointed Saturday morning and drove the forty-five minutes or so to his home, I was not really in the best frame of mind. This couple lived in a part of Charlotte that wasn't a prime target for people in my profession—not exactly the way to build my business, but I did it because I wanted to please the business owner who was an important client. I'm not proud of the resentment I was feeling, but I'm human.

I finally found the road he lived on, rounded a bend, and there it was—a tiny house with a small driveway on a scruffy lot that had never seen a landscaper. As I got out of the car, a very nice young man greeted me warmly and invited me into his home. He led me to their small den where I sat on a small sofa; his wife sat in the only other chair, so he had to bring in a chair from the kitchen. It was one of those hot, sultry days for which North Carolina is well known, but the den window to my left was open allowing a breeze to flow through to the front screen door. Outside the window was a little white German Shepherd puppy with his paws on the sill looking in at these curious people. And as I sat there, feeling the breeze, and watching the puppy, all I could think was, *This is so peaceful. Where is this in my life?* I have to tell you, I was envious. An hour earlier I was thinking how I didn't have time to deal with this family. Now all I wanted was to stay here a little longer.

> *We had the freedom to enjoy life regardless of what we owned or didn't own.*

And it was. Uncomplicated. Simple. Plenty. Even as I write this for you, twenty years after it happened, I can still feel the breeze and see the puppy. I could close my eyes and recall the longing for such a place.

As we got into their financials, I realized that they weren't just starting out even though they lived so modestly. It's just that he didn't make a lot of money and they lived within their means. Because of that, even though they didn't have a lot of income, they had very little debt. They had friends, a place to live, and really seemed to enjoy life together. They were Anne and me many years earlier.

How about you? Are there things you lacked early on that you now have? And what are you missing now that you once had?

Anne and I did not have much when we started together, yet we had something that money couldn't buy. We had the freedom to enjoy life regardless of what we owned or didn't own. We didn't know it at the time, but we were in the garden that God had created for us. We had everything we needed. The voice of the enemy could not be heard above the laughter of our funny Saturday movie nights.

So, yes, there is an enemy that wants to derail God's plans for you and His relationship with you. He will wait for an opportune time (see Luke 4:1-13). But remember, in any battle you face, God and His son have already won the war!

REFLECTION

CHANGE FOR YOUR DOLLAR

1) Creating a home is not about the stuff that fills the space; it's about the love that fills the hearts.
2) Having lots of stuff may offer independence, but it also has the potential to isolate you from community.
3) It is amazing how inventive you become and what you can do without when you have limited resources.
4) Simplicity gives us the freedom to enjoy life regardless of our possessions.

MONEY IN MOTION

1) Reflecting on the early years, think of the "one thing" you miss most and why. If it is possible to get that "one thing" back today, write down some steps to make that happen.
2) If you don't view God as provider of all you have, consider why you struggle with that.
3) Think of an old friend from that time of your life you've lost touch with and why. Take steps to reconnect with them if possible.
4) Look at the ways you compare yourself to others and/or in ways you may compare your old stuff to new stuff—which make you feel content vs. discontent.

PRAYER

Thank you for the fresh start you give us in our lives in you. It's a special time when we learn to love you and love our spouse in the way you intended. As lifestyle creeps into our lives, we desire to be in the world but not of it. Please keep us close so we remain united in our journey. Amen.

living free

Adam and his wife were both naked, and they felt no shame.
—Genesis 2:25

When did you experience the greatest freedom in your adult life? When did you live when you were content in the present and thought little about the future or the past? Whenever that was, I believe you were, in that moment, as close as you could be to living the way God intended for you to live. His plan for all mankind was to create the best place for us to live—a place that contained everything we needed—and then be with us in that beautiful environment. Forever. We wouldn't have to worry about replacing a broken air conditioner because the temperature would be perfect. We wouldn't have to worry about having enough money to pay the bills because there would be no bills. We wouldn't have to worry about food because we would be surrounded by it. With absolutely no reason to worry, we would be free to enjoy our relationship with God and with our neighbors. That was the plan. We might not have been naked, but we didn't have much weighing us down.

The first three words spoken by God to man in Genesis 2:16 were, "You are free..."

The first three words spoken by God to man in Genesis 2:16 were, "You are free . . ."

THE FIRST THREE WORDS

God's intent was for us to be free, and He placed only one restriction on us. To remain free we had to let Him be God, which was really a pretty good deal. Just let God take care of us. He would be the loving, generous, and faithful father from whose hands we could enjoy the riches He had in store for us. As we all know, Adam and Eve blew it—not just for them, but for us as well. Thanks to them, we now have to work, pay bills, save up for college, and constantly worry that we might not have enough. Even then, God had a divine plan. You see, we aren't that different from Adam and Eve. Anne and I blew it. And so have you. God knew we would all blow it. That's why we need His Son.

We equate money with freedom, but we're designed to equate freedom with God.

Can you recall a time in your life when you didn't worry too much about providing the necessities of life? For me, and for most married couples, it was when we had the least money— that period from the honeymoon until the house shrunk. The details may differ, but just about every couple I've worked with has said virtually the same thing about those blissful beginnings: "We didn't have much yet it really didn't seem to matter."

The main reason we look back so fondly on the early years of our marriages is that we were free—as close to Eden that any human could get after the Fall. It's a beautiful irony, really. We tend to think that in order to be truly free, we need to win the lottery or inherit millions from a rich uncle or discover an oil well on our property. Then we can pay all our bills and never have to think twice about buying all the things we want. We equate money with freedom, but we're designed to equate freedom with

God. For most of us, the common denominator of those "good old days," is freedom, not money. In fact, you likely make a lot more money today than when you were first married. Your wealth may be far greater, but are you living free?

Living free works for awhile, but it eventually comes to an end as the result of our wanting something we can't have. Wanting it so badly we'll easily set aside our good judgment and do whatever it takes to get it. God told Adam and Eve they could have anything in the Garden except one thing. And it was that one thing they couldn't have that led to their (and our) downfall. If you want to begin to understand why you may not be living as free as you'd like, go back to that one thing. Go back to where the want began. And from there, go to the next thing you wanted. And then the next. And then the next. Our desires and resulting financial choices tend to compound over time like layers of paint on an antique chair. Sooner or later, you may want to sand it all down and get to the bare wood and start free of old decisions.

> *Living free usually begins out of necessity.*

Living free usually begins out of necessity. When you don't have much, you are not encumbered by your possessions. For some couples, this could last for one, two, three years or more, as it did for Anne and me. Others blow through this period of freedom in a few months. A lot depends on how you were raised, the income from your first job, how you saw your parents managing money, and whether or not you had much as a child. But however long this lasts, you will look back on it and think:

- *Times were special*
- *We were surrounded by community*
- *Life was simpler*
- *We were united in our marriage*
- *Our family was closer*
- *Relationships were rich*

- *A little was a lot*
- *Worries about our financial future were light years away*

We didn't know it at the time, or couldn't articulate it as well, but we were following God's teaching:

You, my brothers and sisters, were called to be free. But do not use your freedom to indulge the flesh; rather, serve one another humbly in love. For the entire law is fulfilled in keeping this one command: "Love your neighbor as yourself."
—Galatians 5:13-14

What we had was each other, some friends, and little to get in the way of either. I wasn't much of a believer then, but God was there. Even those who don't know Christ experience this freedom because they are forced by their circumstances to enjoy God's intention that they be free. Call it divine stupidity, but we didn't know any better than to live out Christ's call to live for free.

THE PRICE OF FREEDOM

Going way back into the Old Testament in the book of Exodus 20:23 we find where Moses climbed Mt. Sinai to be with God. One of the first things God said to him was, "Tell the Israelites this . . . Do not make any gods to be alongside me; do not make for yourselves gods of silver or gods of gold."

Moses spent an extended period on the mountain because God was giving him instructions on how the Israelites should live, including specific plans for how the tabernacle should be built, how they were to observe the Sabbath, and more. Although, for the Hebrew people waiting below, the "good old days" of depending on God, were becoming a distant memory. Where manna and quail once were enough, their appetites grew richer. They were no longer poor, nor did they have to work so hard. They just had to follow what God had asked of them. Simple, right?

They had nothing but time on their hands along with a vast abundance of wealth that had been plundered from Egypt. Free time and wealth are often a deadly combination. With an abundance of both, the Israelites grew restless, and were no longer satisfied with what they had. They wanted more. God had cared for them quite well up to

> *Free time and wealth are often a deadly combination.*

that point. But they thought maybe if they had their own god they could have not just what they needed, but also what they wanted. "Come, make us gods," they demanded of Aaron, the right-hand man of Moses. So he called the Israelites together and told them to remove all their gold jewelry, which he molded into a golden calf—their new god. All it took was a little time, an abundance of resources, a dash of unrest, and misused skills and they had the necessary ingredients for a deadly cocktail of disobedience.

It's counterintuitive, but there's something about dependence that frees us. The converse is also true, especially when it comes to our money. The more we have, the more it enslaves us because it tends to make us less dependent on God. Remember, God desires for us to be free and has given us clear teaching about how we can enjoy that freedom. Surrender to me. Obey me. Trust me. Serve others. Love your neighbor. When we're starting out, we generally do this out of ignorant bliss. Like Adam and Eve, we

> *It's counterintuitive, but there's something about dependence that frees us.*

hear a voice, make a choice, take a bite of the apple in front of us, and then discover that we're naked. We need clothes now. In one "bite," our perspective has changed and we have not become like God at all. All of a sudden we're aware of our needs, where before, it was okay to be naked. Or to put it in more contemporary terms, our Casio was just fine until we saw a guy wearing an Apple watch. Manna was fine, but a thick steak would be even better. Theodore

Roosevelt stated this so clearly when he said, "Comparison is the thief of joy."

It's not about the money. It's not about the stuff. It's the condition of our heart and what we choose to substitute for God and His plans for us. Of course, none of us is ready to cop to idolatry. Instead, we use reason and logic to explain how we went from living free as newlyweds to being frustrated over what's happening to our money. A new car instead of a used car is cheaper in the long run because you won't be wasting all that money on repairs. As you're about to make the final payment on that first brand new car, you reason that instead of another new Ford, you will make a better impression on your clients if you buy something a little classier. Ditto on the house—successful executives don't live here. We need to move over there. Suddenly, your car payments and mortgage are much more than what they were. You wind up spending a little more on new furniture and a lot more on a landscaping service because no one seems to mow their own lawns in this development. What was once a mirage is now becoming a reality, with all that includes.

In fact, no one seems to do anything together in this development. Remember when every weekend you all got together and have some fun grilling or playing some games? And it was not just on the Fourth of July, but just about every Friday and Saturday night. You now have a bigger house, a nicer car, plenty of room to entertain, but you haven't gotten to know your neighbors yet. Besides, you're working sixty hours a week, driving kids to their school and church activities, entertaining clients, or trying to get to the golf course —not so much because you enjoy it, but because you're paying a lot to belong to that club so you better use it. Is the extra money worth the extra stress?

THE REST OF THE STORY

I've had money conversations with thousands of people. And

inevitably I find the same misconceptions. One of the great money myths is that more money = more freedom. A corollary to that myth is that more free time = more freedom. In reality, whenever we have too little or too much of something, it creates a situation that keeps us thinking and focusing on those things. This can distract

> *One of the great money myths is that more money = more freedom.*

us from the true freedom that God intended for us. We either look backward with regret or forward with concern instead of being joyful in the now; yet that is exactly what God asks of us. "Trust me and follow me this day and you will be content." Solomon had some thoughts on this in Proverbs 30:7-9:

> *Two things I ask of you, Lord; do not refuse me before I die: Keep falsehood and lies far from me; give me neither poverty nor riches, but give me only my daily bread. Otherwise, I may have too much and disown you and say, "Who is the Lord?" Or I may become poor and steal and so dishonor the name of my God.*

The problem doesn't lie in how much money or time we have, but in using those resources the way God intended. Okay, I realize that sounds good—even wonderfully Christian—but what exactly does that mean? How can I live for free regardless of how much or how little money I have? The easy—and correct—answer is that we need to learn to be good stewards of all that God has given us. I don't know about you, but I yawn whenever someone mentions stewardship, so to help us get our heads around this biblical concept I want us dig into this directive. Stewardship is a common theme throughout the Bible and each of these stories have the same characteristics. I like to think of them as "stewardship specs." We'll unpack this further in subsequent chapters, but here's how it looks in simple terms:

Master/Owner. God owns everything. We don't own that house, car, clothes, etc. God does. "In the beginning, God created the heavens and the earth" (Genesis 1:1). "The earth is the LORD's, and everything in it, / the world, and all who live in it" (Deuteronomy 10:14).

Mission/Instructions. We have an assignment that transcends our careers or vocations. As Christ-followers, we each have a common calling, an avocation, "Therefore go and make disciples . . . " (Matthew 28:19).

Resources. God has blessed us with an abundance of resources to help us carry out His mission. God (Exodus 3:14), Holy Spirit (Isaiah 55:7-9), Jesus (John 3:16), the Church (Ephesians 2:19-22), the Bible (2 Timothy 3:15-17), Prayer (Matthew 6:5-13), Time (Ecclesiastes 3:1-8), Intellect (Philippians 4:8), Heart (Proverbs 4:23), Body (Genesis 1:27), Talents (1 Corinthians 12:4-6), Creation (Genesis 1:1), Relationships (Philippians 2:3-5), Wealth (Ecclesiastes 5:19)

Steward. That's you (Matthew 25:14-30). What kind of servants will we be?

Choice. You were given the awesome gift of freedom. How will you use it (Proverbs 8:10-11)?

Results/Accountability. Living free isn't accidental. It's the result of your choices (1 Corinthians 3:8-9).

Reward. There are temporary, earthly rewards and eternal, heavenly rewards. (Colossians 3:23-24). We may not know what the reward will be but with God you know it will be incredible!

Enemy. "The devil made me do it" only happens if we let him.

Financial problems are usually spiritual problems in disguise (1 Peter 5:8-9).

Now let's look at these "stewardship specs" in the context of a well-known passage of scripture—the Parable of the Talents in Matthew 25:14-30:

For it will be like a man (*master/owner*) going on a journey, who called his servants (*steward*) and entrusted to them (*mission/instructions*) his property. To one he gave five talents, (*resources*) to another two, to another one, to each according to his ability. Then he went away.

He who had received the five talents went at once and traded with them (*choice*), and he made five talents more. So also he who had the two talents made (*choice*) two talents more. But he who had received the one talent went and dug in the ground (*choice*) and hid his master's money. Now after a long time the master of those servants came and settled accounts with them. (*results/accountability*) And he who had received the five talents came forward, bringing five talents more, saying, "Master, you delivered to me five talents; here I have made five talents more." His master said to him, "Well done, good and faithful servant. You have been faithful over a little; I will set you over much. (*reward*) Enter into the joy of your master."

And he also who had the two talents came forward, saying, "Master, you delivered to me two talents; here I have made two talents more." His master said to him, "Well done, good and faithful servant. You have been faithful over a little; I will set you over much. (*reward*) Enter into the joy of your master." He also who had received the one talent came forward, saying, "Master, I knew you to be a hard man, reaping where you did not sow, and gathering where you scattered no seed, so I was afraid, (*enemy*) and I went and hid your talent in the ground. Here you have what is yours."

But his master answered him, "You wicked and slothful servant! You knew that I reap where I have not sown and gather where I scattered no seed? Then you ought to have invested my money with the bankers, and at my coming I should have received what was my own with interest. (*results/accountability*) So take the talent from him and give it to him who has the ten talents. For to everyone who has will more be given, and he will have an abundance. (*reward*) But from the one who has not, even what he has will be taken away. (*results/accountability*) And cast the worthless servant into the outer darkness. In that place there will be weeping and gnashing of teeth."

Those are the "specs" in the stewardship story. It's our story. It's Anne and me. It's your spouse and you. You can find many stories in the Bible with these same components at work. Each is important. Each needs to be addressed and understood because they all will ultimately come to bear in our own stories. I find that knowing who and what is involved can lead us to make much better financial decisions.

Unfortunately, it's an enemy that often gets us into trouble. "*Did he really say. . .*" The enemy's whisper beckons us to fear, worry, and want. A whisper in your ear comes to tell you something is out there that you need—that God is holding out on you with His blessings. Someone else has something, and if they have it, you need it too. The house that once seemed more than enough for you, became too small, unattractive, and inadequate as soon as one of your neighbors moves to a better neighborhood.

Yes, God's first words spoken to man were, "You are free." And Jesus gave his life so we could be free. "*It is for freedom that Christ has set us free*" (Galatians 5:1). But in that same passage is the rest of the story: "... do not use your freedom to indulge the sinful nature." Having a nice house, an expensive car, family vacations are not sins . . . until they are. When they gradually insert themselves between you and God. It doesn't happen overnight, nor do we consciously turn them into idols. I don't know anyone who declared, "Today I have decided to worship my possessions."

It sneaks up on us. We don't see it coming, and more often than not, we aren't even aware that it happened. It's like a short text when driving. We know it's dangerous, but we do it anyway. Then the text messages get longer and then an accident occurs. Everything is fine, until it's not. Remember, the enemy is patient. He waits for an opportune time. And then he whispers to you a message, a flaming arrow that strikes to your heart: "You deserve more."

REFLECTION

CHANGE FOR YOUR DOLLAR

1) God wants us to live for free, but what we think of as free, often does not align with God's idea of free.
2) The greatest liberation we experience is discovering that depending on God releases us from our burdens.
3) Stewardship isn't just a word used to encourage offerings in church. It is the fabric of how you handle all of the resources God gave you to live all of the life God has planned for you.
4) God's intention is for us to experience freedom, but the enemy's intention is for us to be bound by our possessions.

MONEY IN MOTION

1) Think of two words—a verb and a noun—to describe

what it means for you to "live for free."

2) Try to recall a favorite "no money" date with your spouse that you used to enjoy and what made it so special. Set a date to do it again sometime soon.

3) If you have found that money provides more opportunities for worship or more opportunities for distraction, please describe your experience.

4) Write down what you think God meant when he said "You are free."

PRAYER

Lord, you had a simple plan for Adam and Eve and I know you have a simple plan for me. Your gifts are always good but I don't always use them the way you have asked. Even your best gifts can be used to imprison me in little or big ways when I don't follow you. I want to follow you. I want to live with abandon with you as my focus. I want to live for free. Amen.

wanting more

Now the serpent was more crafty than any of the wild animals the Lord God had made. He said to the woman, "Did God really say, 'You must not eat from any tree in the garden'?" The woman said to the serpent, "We may eat fruit from the trees in the garden, but God did say, 'You must not eat fruit from the tree that is in the middle of the garden, and you must not touch it, or you will die.'" "You will not certainly die," the serpent said to the woman. "For God knows that when you eat from it your eyes will be opened, and you will be like God, knowing good and evil."
—Genesis 3:1-5

We had everything we needed. I had a good job, a nice home with a low mortgage, a new car, three kids. Anne had been teaching, so we had a little extra money. Then my salary started to increase, so Anne was able to do what she really wanted, which was to stay home with the kids. With the savings from not having our kids in childcare every week, we only "lost" a few hundred dollars a month. My job was demanding, but not in an oppressive way. I had some flexibility, so I could be around in the morning when the kids got up. I was able to play some golf with a client. Anne and I could go to the movies, and we graduated from Subway to Chili's. I mean, think about it—from bologna to Subway to Chili's. Could it get any better? Life was good. We were living free.

A COSTLY PROPOSITION

One day, a friend of mine invited me to join him and one of his friends for lunch. I knew his friend, but not very well. He owned his own business and seemed to be fairly successful. After ordering lunch, we engaged in some small talk and the business owner asked me where I lived.

"We were one of the first to buy a house in Bedford Crest," I proudly told him.

His answer literally changed the financial trajectory of my life at that time.

"Oh really? Nobody who's successful lives in Bedford Crest."

It was more than the enemy's whisper of desire; this time it came with a dagger.

Somewhat defensively I explained that we had made a lot of improvements to our place, that our lot was one of the bigger ones, and that I had gotten it at such a great price I would be stupid to move. But deep down inside I knew. I was successful in the best possible ways, but I wanted others to view me

> It was more than the enemy's whisper of desire; this time it came with a dagger.

as successful as well. I wanted more. "Nobody who's successful lives in Bedford Crest." The dagger had hit its mark. I had to get out of there.

Up until that point, I loved our little home. It had everything we needed. But from that moment, I began to see it differently. Ours was the seventh house to be built in what eventually became a development of hundreds of homes. You entered the neighborhood, turned right, and the first right was our cul-de-sac. If you turned left after entering the neighborhood, you were in a section of newer homes that were noticeably nicer and larger with bigger lots. I'd never really thought much about it, but now whenever I told someone where I lived, I knew why they had asked,

"Do you turn right or left?" Right meant the less expensive homes, left the classier ones. It never bothered me before, but now it did. It wasn't so much that I didn't like our house. After all of these years, I admit this to you; what I really wanted was a place that would have a stronger impact on what people thought about me.

> The enemy planted a seed of doubt, a seed of discontent. Then bent God's word's ever so slightly. He does the same thing today.

After his rather rude comment, the business owner then went on to describe how he had just moved to a place that had a clubhouse, a pool, tennis courts, and bigger houses. Of course. He was a successful business owner. He lived in a place that he believed communicated success to others, and that's what I wanted. In an instant, I went from hero to zero. From being content, to the unrest of wanting more. I mistakenly listened to a whisper of desire that made perfect sense because the enemy was patient and came to me at the most opportune time in the most opportune way. Remember in Eden when the serpent appeared to Eve? He didn't begin by telling her to disobey God. Instead, he simply raised a question: "Did God really say ...?" He planted a seed of doubt, a seed of discontent. Then bent God's words ever so slightly. He does the same thing today.

I knew in my heart that we lived in a perfectly adequate house, and the enemy never really criticized our house. Instead, he planted a seed in the fertile soil of my ambitious desires. *Your place is fine*, he said calmly. *Nothing wrong with it. Except. "No one who's successful lives there."* The daggers of the enemy are flaming lies and designed to wound. I knew for a fact there were successful people in our neighborhood, and I'm sure there still are. Even so, it penetrated just the way it was intended. He hit me at the core of my beliefs and doubts and misplaced desires for acceptance. He hit me with the future of my business. He used my behavior against me. He knew I craved success and the approval of others, and it got my attention. It was as if a light switch flipped to on in my very being. Let the striving begin.

THE COMPARISON TRAPS

In hindsight, I can see that perception pattern began as a teenager. I'm the youngest of five boys and even though we didn't have a lot, we had all we needed. Now, if you are a "little brother" or "little sister" you have likely experienced the hand-me-down scenario. I didn't own a new piece of clothing until I was in high school! Okay,

> *What I had was functional, but it wasn't fashionable.*

that may be a little bit of an exaggeration . . . but not much. The wardrobes of my older brothers were Mom's shopping mall. She was frugal and she was right. My Wranglers were fine, but would a new pair of Levi's break the bank? All it takes is for a little comparison and desire to sneak in and all of a sudden what I had was not good enough. What I had was functional, but it wasn't fashionable—just like my house in Bedford Crest.

We want others to see us as successful, right? But it was different this time. The stakes were higher. It was no longer about wearing the right jeans to the high school party—that's a $30 problem. Now, we were into a multi-six-figure decision and it would affect my whole family. Once again, my money and I were a dangerous duo.

Over a routine business lunch with someone I barely knew, I let the enemy's whisper reach my unprepared heart and made the irrational leap from living free to wanting more.

So, home I went to inform Anne that we needed to move. It wasn't too hard to convince a woman raising three young children in a 1,800 square foot house that we needed more space. My rationalization was that business was on the upswing, and we needed to grow with it. Everything would be okay. She believed me. I believed me. Salesmen are always the easiest marks, especially when they're selling themselves on an idea.

Soon after, we moved into a new house in a neighborhood with a more prestigious address. And of course our old furniture—which up until then had been just fine—had to be replaced with furniture more appropriate for the style of house we had chosen. The brown sofa had to go. As this was happening, I picked up a couple of new clients, which increased our cash flow and I remember thinking, *Wow! Now we can afford to start looking like we're more successful.* So we began buying things that added to the image I was creating: oriental rugs, matching furniture for the sunroom, and of course a top-of-the-line security system to protect all the stuff we began accumulating. And guess what? Despite making more money than I had ever made before, we weren't any better off. Where before we never really thought that much about money, it was beginning to be consuming. Now it created tension, worry. I felt trapped because I had to work harder just to keep up. We used to have a little extra money to fall back on if we needed it, but now we were living close to the edge.

I remember not being able to sleep one night and just pacing the halls of our new house wondering, *What in the world have I done?* Buyer's remorse. Has that ever happened to you? I knew I should have stayed where we could afford to live more freely. While my family slept that night, I found myself restless with anxiety. I found my way downstairs into my new study and pulled out a blank notebook, and here is what I wrote in those early morning hours so many years ago:

> *It's 12:15 am. Anne and the kids are asleep. I just got home from a trip yesterday. I woke up in an anxious panic worrying about debt, money, my business, my overspending (my weakness). I've been reading Philippians 4:4-20. My heart's focus is not on God, it's on me, what I can do, and the stuff I can buy, and how I can look better than I am to the outside world. I had made a note in my Bible study that said, "Don't try to change*

your behavior when the issue is your heart." I remember when I asked Christ to enter my life and save me. Since then I have felt a closeness to God, and at the same time, like a tug of war, my focus shifts to the outside world. I prayed tonight for God to change my heart toward him and help me to focus on what I can do for Him, not on what I want. I don't ever want to forget the fear, the panic, the anxiety that tonight brought. Yes, I do have debt that I should not have. Tonight that stops. No more will I be slave to my earthly desires. God has shifted my heart's focus tonight and I want it shifted for good to God and His will for me. I will not sabotage God's plan for me, my family, and my business any more! Today marks a victory for God in my life and my heart. "In God I trust, I will not be afraid!"

Soon after I wrote this, by God's provision, our situation stabilized. What a relief I felt. That is until one of my buddies in our neighborhood moved into an even pricier development. Pretty soon the new friends I had made in this neighborhood were putting their houses up for sale. You'd think I would have learned. You would think I would have remembered my journal entry from a few years before, the sleepless nights, and the pain I felt. But once you build that barrier—that disconnect—between God's provision and your own desires, it's like the dominoes falling all over again. One unwise choice often leads to another.

It's not as though I turned my back on God. I was still active in church, spent time in the Bible most days, and tried to live a disciplined life. Whenever my salary increased, I believed God was blessing me. What I didn't realize at the time is that every financial decision we make takes us either closer to, or further from, our God. I was using His provision for my own needs, not to serve Him and others. And one of my needs was fueled by comparison. If one of my buddies moved to a bigger house, mine was inferior by comparison; and to me, that also meant I was inferior. That's worldly math. Through this experience, I witnessed once again that comparison destroys contentment, and then creates it. (At least for a little while.)

Have you ever noticed that? If you're like me, the desire for the acceptance and approval of others is an ongoing journey. The train never stops for long. When I sense that something else may make me appear better than I am, I will want to implement it, sometimes at the expense of being financially responsible. Then think once I am "there," with my new self on display, I look around at others like me and I have "arrived." The comparison that once destroyed my contentment now creates it. That is, until I see the next thing that is supposed to enhance my façade. Welcome to my world. The approval train slowed down for a moment, but it didn't stop.

Do you remember your first car? It could have been a junker, but to you it was so much better than walking, it might as well have been a Rolls Royce. Then one of your buddies drove into the school parking lot with cool pick-up truck—no rust, oversized tires. To become content, you had to upgrade. And it worked. The comparison that first created the discontent was now the comparison that created comfort and complacency. You now belong because that truck you bought made you feel great, made you feel you were in the "cool car club" . . . until another kid bought a convertible. Contentment destroyed.

And to make it even more powerful, the comparison trap is not about only looking around at others and what they have and comparing your stuff to theirs. It's also looking around at what else is available for me that is "better" than what I already have. It's about my desire and my discontent. It's a cycle that fuels our economy. Why do you think they open malls at 6:00 a.m. for walkers? They know that if you walk past all of those gorgeous things in the windows, the stuff you have will not look quite as good. It's the best advertising retailers could ask for. Yes, you will leave the mall after your walk, but the images won't leave your mind. To reveal the secret the retailers know about mall-walkers, let me tweak a phrase from everybody's favorite *Terminator*, Arnold Schwarzenegger, "You'll be back."

So, this comparison trap led us (me) to buy our third house, and it was in pretty rough shape—vintage 1965—but I thought we could afford to have it completely remodeled. Then I lost a major client and our income took a nosedive. So now we were living in a shabby house in a gorgeous neighborhood, and life was really closing in on us. Living free seemed so far away from us. I was living in

> *Comparison is always about me; contentment is always about Christ.*

"wanting more mode." It is a pattern that I see repeated every day by wonderful Christian families who love the Lord and want to live for Him.

I found another entry from one of my journals from that time in my life, and it read something like this:

> *We just moved into a new house ($$). It's going to need some work ($$). The kids are in a private Christian school ($$). And then there's our lifestyle ($$). All this creates a large financial need and asking God for guidance.*

The money myth was alive and well: *If I just had more money, everything would be better.* Somehow in my daily reading of the Bible, I missed a passage that described this pattern with remarkable clarity:

> *Now listen, you who say, "Today or tomorrow we will go to this or that city, spend a year there, carry on business and make money." Why, you do not even know what will happen tomorrow. What is your life? You are a mist that appears for a little while and then vanishes. Instead, you ought to say, "If it is the Lord's will, we will live and do this or that." As it is, you boast in your arrogant schemes.*

All such boasting is evil. If anyone, then, knows the good
they ought to do and doesn't do it, it is sin for them.
—James 4: 13-17

I put my trust in more—and more proved to be a lousy savior. Don't get me wrong; more isn't automatically bad. The Bible is filled with wealthy families—godly men and women He entrusted with great wealth and they used it for God's purposes. By the same token, less isn't automatically good. The Bible also warns us and introduces us to people who were poor, or misguided, and just as with the steward in the parable of the talents, who didn't make good use of the little he had.

> *I put my trust in more—*
> *and more proved to*
> *be a lousy saviour*

Some Christians consider wealth a sign that God is pleased with you. That if you put your trust in God He will make you rich. This is sometimes referred to as "prosperity gospel." Others believe that if you're truly godly you will get rid of everything but the bare necessities, wearing plain clothes and living in humble houses. As with a lot of ideas, there is truth in both, but I prefer to think of God as provision: *"God who richly provides us with everything . . ."* (1 Timothy 6:17) Whether you have a lot or a little, it all comes from God. How we use what He has given us determines whether it is a blessing or a curse. If we use our "riches" only for ourselves, we will not experience the blessings—living for free—that God intended for us. Blessings from God's perspective are designed to be used for His plans on earth. If we use his provision only for ourselves, no matter how much we have, we will never be content.

> *How we use what He*
> *has given us determines*
> *whether it is a blessing*
> *or a curse.*

FINANCIAL FORENSICS

Financial forensics is my method designed to understand what is involved in a financial choice and hopefully help find the root of the underlying financial and spiritual issues. It's especially useful for any financial problem that continues to repeat itself causing concern. I believe you will find this incredibly valuable as we continue to look at our stewardship choices around finances.

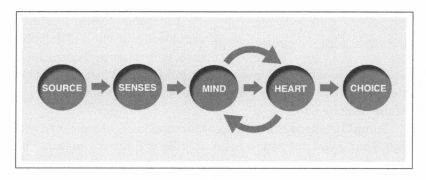

It's very basic in design and follows what we each deal with when presented with any question or opportunity that requires action. We all make thousands of choices every day. Some are very fast, while some take more time. There is always a *source* of the question or choice, and we experience that through one or more of our five *senses* (see, hear, smell, touch, feel). That information then travels to our *mind* to think about and sometimes on to our *heart* to compare to what we believe. This *mind/heart* cycle can spin for a while depending on the situation at hand and any conflicts that arise. It probably goes something like this: *In my* mind *I want to do it, but in my* heart, *I know I shouldn't.* Let me add a quick insight. If the *mind* and the *heart* ever get into a disagreement, the *mind* can win, temporarily, through willpower, but eventually, the *heart* and your beliefs always prevail. Finally, after the question leaves the *mind/heart* cycle, you get to make your *choice*. Let me share a little more detail about each of the steps:

SOURCE – This is where any opportunity, question, or message originates from, and every *source* has it's own motives and messages. A simple example of a *source* is advertising. Advertising has a motive—*to sell you*—and a marketing message—*to disturb you*. They are positioning their message aimed at a *trigger*, and if they hit it, they are likely to win you over. I'm sure you will not be surprised when I tell you that *source* motives can be negative or positive. They can be of the world or they can be of Christ. In addition, the messages from these motives can be disguised to appear positive, when they are not good for you at all. Fortunately, we know that Christ is the ultimate source of all truth.

> *Jesus answered, "I am the way and the truth and the life.*
> *No one comes to the Father except through me."*
> —John 14:6

SENSES – God designed our five senses to allow us to see, hear, smell, taste, and touch the world around us that He created. Every sense is an outlet for experiencing our surroundings and internalizing the situations and messages aimed at us. To guard our heart means also to guard our *senses* and what we let into our minds. Sometimes that will mean closing our eyes and our ears to worldly influences around us. Therefore, if we can minimize unwanted input, we can maximize desired output.

> *Ears that hear and eyes that see -*
> *the Lord has made them both.*
> —Proverbs 20:12

MIND – God has given us the ability to learn, think and reason. Our mind and its respective thoughts are powerful and creative. We also have incredible freedom with our mind, how we use it and what we think about. Negative thoughts and lies from the enemy can derail our lives for years, while positive thoughts and truths from God can strengthen our minds, and enable us to change the world. We should be diligent in mastering our minds for Him.

Finally, brothers and sisters, whatever is true, whatever is noble, whatever is right, whatever is pure, whatever is lovely, whatever is admirable—if anything is excellent or praiseworthy—think about such things.
—Philippians 4:8

HEART – Our hearts house our beliefs and our behaviors. They hold love, hate, or a multitude of other powerful directives. What ultimately shapes our hearts is a massive combination of all the input and observations of our lives. Once these beliefs are formed, it can be difficult, but not impossible, to change them. The choice we make is guided by our hearts, and our desire is that our heart and what "flows from it" will be of God. Therefore, my friend Ron Blue's thoughts on this topic are important and appropriate. "There are no financial choices, only spiritual choices." We should rest in the truth that only God can change our *heart*, but we should be resolute in the protection of it, because it affects all that we are and all that we do.

> *There are no financial choices, only spiritual choices.*

Above all else, guard your heart, for everything you do flows from it.
—Proverbs 4:23

CHOICE – After we understand the situation or opportunity at hand, and after we have time to think about it in our minds and wrestle with it in our hearts, it's time to make a CHOICE. This is a perfect time to submit to prayer all you are considering, with what you know and believe about the situation. Prayer is one of the most underutilized and most powerful resources we have at our daily disposal. Let God guide your *choice* through prayer and let His word fill your mind and heart, and you will have the best opportunity to make a *choice* that pleases your audience of One.

> *Who, then, are those who fear the Lord?*
> *He will instruct them in the ways they should choose.*
> *—Psalm 25:12*

Using the "Financial Forensics" formula you can retrace a decision or you can use it to get very clear understanding of a choice. Let me show you how it works by retracing a choice we made to move from a perfectly good house, in a beautiful neighborhood, for all the wrong reasons. A downloadable form can be found on www.JohnHPutnam.com.

FINANCIAL FORENSICS FORMULA

SOURCE

Someone I did not know well made a simple statement expressing his own opinion. It might be considered a rude comment, but I don't believe there was any malice intended. It did resonate from a sense of pride because he lived in a "nicer" neighborhood, which means this message was coming from a worldly perspective. That should have been caution flag #1.

SENSES

We were eating lunch together having general conversation and small talk. I heard the comment. That was it. No other influencers from anything in my environment.

MIND

I had never even contemplated this idea. Bedford Crest was a great neighborhood. I knew "successful" people who lived there. Did "people" think this was a neighborhood of average achievers? It brought into question my appearance of success. Yet another worldly perspective. Caution flag #2.

HEART

It really did not matter what I knew to be true. In my heart, I was insecure and wanted the applause of others. I wanted the perception of worldly success. *Big* caution flag # 3. This was more important to me than a wise decision. If we could figure out how to afford it, we were going to move.

My CHOICE is/was...

I decided to sell our smaller house and move to a larger house in a "perceived" nicer neighborhood.

Anne will tell you that we would not have stayed in that neighborhood forever, and she is once again, probably right. The point to the above *financial forensics* is that the desire to move and the reason to move at that specific money moment was prompted by a worldly perspective and a confused heart. The results may have been different if I had been a more mature follower of Christ, or if I had a support system around me. Regardless, it's part of our story and possibly for the reason to be able to explore it and share it with you today.

If I were to perform some additional *financial forensics* on my past choices, I could trace many of my poor money decisions back to one perception—a lie—that appealed to a driving force in my life: the appearance of success. I was vulnerable to the enemy's whisper for a number of reasons. First, I had been leaning in that

direction since high school. I had been like a car out of alignment for along time, and if I took my hands off the steering wheel, I would begin to veer off course.
I had little or no godly counsel on my team. There was no one I invited to speak truth to me regularly and minimal

> *Success is having what you want. Joy is wanting what you've been given.*

accountability. Instead, the players on my team were worry and want—worry over what people might think of me if I stayed in our little house and want to acquire things that would help me create a perception of success. In addition, having been in sales for a very long time. I have found (not a scientific study) that the more of my human senses (sight, smell, hear, taste, touch) that are firing when choices are made, the easier it is for me to make a poor decision. I heard the whisper, took the bait, and I chose poorly. Tough combo.

What I didn't realize at the time is this: Success is having what you want. Joy is wanting what you've been given.

If you're experiencing stress about money issues, I can almost guarantee that it's because you're in, or have been in, the "wanting more" mode. And I can also predict that you may likely disagree with me, because of the insidious nature of more.

There will be some reading this who have experienced, or are experiencing, financial difficulties due to situations beyond their control such as an accident, illness, or some other unforeseen tragedy. I am so sorry if you have suffered a financial setback not of your own doing. These hazards occur at different levels in each of our lives. That's not what I'm talking about here. I am talking about those of us who have financial options and the ability to choose, yet still choose poorly.

THE HEART OF THE MATTER

There were many times I knew in my head that I was about to make a poor money choice, but my heart convinced me to continue. At one time we found a house we really wanted, but it was just out of our price range. A friend of mine was the builder and really wanted me to have that house, but after running the numbers one last time, I had to be honest with him. "Tim, we love the house, but I just can't afford it," I told him over the phone.

> *The power of more can cloud our better judgment, convincing us we can have what we want.*

"John, is it the price of the house that you can't afford or the monthly payments?" he responded.

I told him the monthly payments on the mortgage were just too much. The payment exceeded what the bank determined I could afford to qualify for the mortgage. And I should have just walked away from the deal. But my answer gave him—and me—an opening.

"John, if I can structure this so you can qualify you at that monthly payment, are you in?"

I said, "Sure!," listening to my heart instead of my head.

I then began rationalizing what was clearly a bad money decision. The power of more can cloud our better judgment, convincing us we can have what we want. It's what causes friction in relationships when a spouse asks, "Are you sure we can afford this?" But, you know what? We could. "It's gonna be a little tight for a while," I explained. "But I've got a little more money coming in this year. We're buying low, so it's a good investment. We'll be fine." Once again, I was making dangerous presumptions about the future, and spending based on that. My trust was in the economy, not the God of provision. I call this the male veil, an overconfidence in ourselves as husbands and providers, and we all do it: "It's gonna be okay, sweetheart." And we are drawn deeper and deeper into the mirage, losing sight of reality and what lies beneath our choices.

Wanting more has little to do with money and plenty to do with what really drives you. For most men, the desire for success is at the root, and that shouldn't surprise us. What are we taught from day one? Go get an education and make something of your life. Success can be a good thing. I thought I was doing what any decent man would do, and I often used that to justify my financial decisions. I was providing for Anne and the kids, giving them opportunities to grow and learn. But instead of listening to the still, small voice of God that said, "Trust me," I listened to the whisper that said "More."

For many women, the need to feel secure is a motivating force. "Are we going to be okay?" We shouldn't be surprised here either. Women tend to be nurturers and protectors in their families, which is a good thing. Women are so often the anchor of the family, the powerful heart that guides and encourages the journey. But sometimes God doesn't guide the way we want, and we think maybe He needs a little help. We may need to hold onto a little bit more. In either case, the temptation is to trust me rather than Thee.

Wanting more has little to do with money and plenty to do with what really drives you.

If you find yourself in the "wanting more" mode, you're not alone. Most of us move between living free and wanting more. There will be times when your financial picture is bright, you are content with what you have, and you are able to ignore the voice that is always there. Always. There also will be times when you take a bite out of the apple. All of your five senses fire at once—you *see* what you want, you *hear* the voice of desire, you *smell* the fruit, you *feel* the smooth skin, then finally, you take a *bite*. You never stand a chance on your own.

The enemy is as cunning as he is patient. He understands so clearly how more can create a distraction—build a barrier—between God and us. His goal is to separate us from Christ and take what He has given us. He will dangle in front of you whatever he believes will attract you, always at the opportune time, and money is simple and abundant bait. The only guard against the enemy's distraction is a stronger attraction.

More than 400 years ago, the great poet John Milton answered his previous poem, *Paradise Lost*, with *Paradise Regained*.

> *The enemy is as cunning as he his patient*

In it, he recounted the temptation of Jesus in the wilderness, suggesting that innocence can be reclaimed. With all due respect to Milton, I'm not sure we can actually return to Eden this side of heaven. According to the Bible, we are cursed by the sin of Adam and will never return to the total freedom experienced in Eden while living in this world. But God still desires for us to live free. And the good news is we can.

REFLECTION

CHANGE FOR YOUR DOLLAR

1) No matter how content you are with your current situation, comparison will always cause you to grow dissatisfied quickly.
2) It is easy to find a rationalization for any choice if we want it enough.
3) Remember: the enemy is patient and works best when he is sowing the seeds of discord, distraction and discontent.
4) "Freedom to . . ." and "Freedom from . . . " are less about the size of your bank account and more about the scope of your intent.

MONEY IN MOTION

1) If you feel you have gotten ahead of God's plans with your money choices think about how you got there.
2) The enemy looks for "opportune times" to whisper messages designed to interrupt God's plans and take you

off course. Look at your life and identify at least three situations when you believe you are most vulnerable.

3) "Buyer's remorse" is a common feeling. Think about items in question when you've felt this way and consider if that was because the item too nice, too expensive, bought on credit, etc.

4) Describe a current financial choice that needs to be placed into the shadow of the cross and why you feel it needs to be placed there.

PRAYER

I know I can't love you and money. I often have a foot squarely planted in your love and the other foot equally firm in the world. I often fall victim to the enemy's traps. Other times I can make barriers between us from my poor decisions. Help me want you more than I want things. Even though my actions may not show it, I pray to have the courage to choose you over all. Amen.

taking control

When the woman saw that the fruit of the tree was good for food and pleasing to the eye, and also desirable for gaining wisdom, she took some and ate it. She also gave some to her husband, who was with her, and he ate it.
—Genesis 1:27

I have a friend who had a lifelong dream of owning a sailboat—not just a little Hobie Cat or day-sailor he could tow behind his car—a real ocean-going yacht he could live on with his family and maybe cast off to sail around the world. He subscribed to various sailing magazines. He visited marinas, shopping for the perfect boat, wistfully imagining himself at the wheel, and heading out of the harbor into the great beyond. He knew he could never afford to buy a vessel capable of such adventure and vicariously lived out his fantasy by reading about others who sailed to the far corners of the world.

One day as he was scanning the classifieds in the back of one of his sailing magazines, he saw a picture of the boat of his dreams with a price he could hardly believe. For only $17,500 he could own a boat capable of sailing the oceans. Only two things stood in the way: one, he didn't have $17,500; two, the boat's low price reflected its condition. It needed a lot of work, and my friend would be the first to admit he wasn't very handy with tools and knew nothing about restoring a sailboat.

So of course, he bought the boat. He figured he needed to learn how to sail and planned to keep working on the boat as he learned. The marina charged $1,200 to launch and store the boat, and another $1,500 for slip rental. Annually. He was chasing his dream.

Fast forward. The boat, which he purchased with money he took from his 401k, sits in a boatyard. Instead of restoring it to pristine condition and sailing the world, he made a few cosmetic improvements and then had it launched in the bay about an hour-and-a-half from his home.

Unfortunately, he was living his adventure all by himself. 100% alone. His wife didn't enjoy sailing. His teenaged kids were too busy with school and sports activities. Naturally, he felt guilty spending every weekend on his sailboat, but with so much money tied up in his boat, and the added maintenance expenses, he had to get his money's worth. So off he went every weekend, forcing himself to enjoy a dream that was quickly turning into a nightmare. The boat created a heaviness in his life that slowed him down, mentally and emotionally, almost to a point of stagnation. His boat to freedom felt more like an anchor.

One winter, as his boat sat on its $1,200 cradle waiting to be launched in the spring with a $1,500 boost, he and his wife were helping their oldest son fill out college applications, and it just sort of hit him. "Where am I going to find the money to help him pay for college?" That night, as he tried to fall asleep, the reality of his dream became clear:

- This boat is costing us a lot.
- I'm not really enjoying sailing all by myself.
- I'm being selfish to let something that expensive just sit there.
- Because I haven't maintained it well, it's worth less than what I paid for it.
- The annual storage and slip fees alone are the exact additional amount we needed to pay for our son's first year of college.

My friend learned an important lesson about the natural progression of wanting more. At some point, the material possessions or experiences we believe will make life more enjoyable for us can actually make it worse. Instead of giving

> *Everything we buy, whether small or large, can set a hook into our minds and souls.*

us the freedom or pleasure or satisfaction that we expected, they enslave us. Everything we buy, whether small or large, can set a hook into our minds and our souls. As our earning power increases, we have the opportunity to accelerate the options in our lives and we automatically come to a universal fork in the road: Do we follow our plan or God's plan? Or, more accurately, who's going to take control? Who's the captain of this boat? God or me?

WHO'S THE BOSS?

It's kind of like a husband and wife watching television together and the wife has the remote. She's flipping through the channels, stopping every now and then to check something out, and he starts fidgeting. He wants to be considerate and let his wife select the program, but she's not doing it fast enough. So at some point, he gets exasperated. "Honey, will you just give me the remote?"

As our resources present us with increased options, we grab the remote away from God. He's not delivering fast enough. He doesn't know what we really want. He's not stopping on the right channels, or He's on a different wavelength altogether. Actually, that last statement is oh so true.

It's not that we don't appreciate all He has done for us; all He has given us. It's just that we want to be in charge. And what most of us do is convince ourselves that God is blessing our plan by giving us all these wonderful things and experiences. We do it without even thinking. You pull into the church parking lot in a new car and your friends compliment you on the new purchase, and what do you say? "Well, we're just grateful to God for the way He has blessed us."

And for a while it works, thanks to 72 months same as cash. Or for an even faster experience, we tap "BUY" with PayPal and whatever you want is at your door in the morning. We can have something now,

> *Just because you can buy it, doesn't mean you can afford it.*

and pay for it later. We can accelerate our desires and don't have to deal with the cost. That's the trap. We see something we want. We don't have enough money to buy it; but there's always an "affordable plan," which is why we have so much, and why it eventually moves from blessing to curse. Just because you can buy it, doesn't mean you can afford it.

That's the enemy at work. After tempting you with the very thing (or things) he knows you want, he then distracts you from enjoying it, and definitely keeps you from sharing it. My friend and teacher, highly-respected author and financial advisor, Ron Blue, calls this the *Paradox of Prosperity*: "The more you have, the more choices you have and the more confusing life becomes, and the fear of losing it grows stronger."

Isn't that a fascinating perspective? Let it sink in: The one thing you have been dreaming about and planning for is often the very thing that creates a barrier between you and God. And if it can do that, it also has the potential to create a wedge in your next most important relationship—you and your spouse.

Oh, the math works—0% interest is a great deal . . . as long as everything is okay. The job is going well; you are making all those monthly payments; you are healthy, belong to a great church, and host a small group in the "lovely home God provided"—as long as you

> *The one thing you have been dreaming about and planning for is often the very thing that creates a barrier between you and God.*

keep all the plates spinning, it works. But all of this "blessing" feeds upon itself. Your house is nice, but you start thinking about a timeshare for vacations, or maybe even a vacation home. Maybe it's things with wheels and motors or clothes and shoes. For a while, it feels a lot like we're experiencing the "Blessings that crown the head of the righteous" (Proverbs 10:6). God must really be pleased with us to lavish us with such provision. Our perception is not always fact.

I WANT IT MY WAY

Do you remember the stewardship specs? Owner, mission, steward, resources, instructions, choice, results, reward, and an enemy. It's absolutely true that God is providing you with the job, the money, the resources that you have. That part we get. He owns it all, which allows us to get all spiritual about the cool stuff we own. It makes us feel good to acknowledge that God blessed us with a promotion that enabled us to stuff yet another outfit into the closet. It's true.

> *God provides, but we choose.*

God provides, but we choose. In other words, He provides us with resources, but also gives us the freedom to choose what we do with them. And here is the interesting part. The issue is not in the homes, or vacations, or the clothes, or the shoes, or any of the other things we spend money on—that would be much too easy to solve. It's what lies underneath our financial choices. That is the culprit.

It's that control thing. In essence, God's saying, "You can do it your way, or you can do it my way." If we choose to use those resources primarily for our own enjoyment, we eventually experience just the opposite. The man with the boat? He told me that even when he sat in church with his family on Sunday mornings, all he could think about was his boat. How much it demanded of him. How much was costing him. How it was supposed to be fun, but wasn't. What began as an innocent dream became a nightmare because he chose his way, not God's.

A lot of people think stewardship is giving a portion of what *you own* back to God. That if we just give our ten percent to the church, we can have all of our other money and stuff and everything will be fine. But that's only the tithe. What about the other ninety percent? (Or, in reality, the other ninety-seven percent since the average Christian only gives approximately three percent of their incomes to God.) As stewards, we're given the freedom to manage it all, but we're also given instructions *by God* on how He wants us to handle His provision. Let's allow this to sink in for a minute. God provides 100% of our resources to us to use for His glory, to know Him, to make Him known, and love our neighbor as ourselves, but our average personal overhead is running at about 97%. What's wrong with that picture? Stewardship is every choice you make after you've said "yes" to Jesus. Everything we do with everything we have is to bring Him glory. When our desire for Him exceeds our desire for anything else, our money problems begin to fade.

> *When our desire for Him exceeds our desire for anything else, our money problems begin to fade.*

FALSE FREEDOM

So why do so many of us who love Christ find ourselves struggling with money issues? We take control over our resources because we want the freedom we believe it promises. If we relinquish control of our finances to God, He might not let us have what we want. But in reality, when we take control we actually give up our freedom because our possessions take control of us. Or let me put it a different way, when we pursue our own idea of freedom, we create our own prison. You join a country club because you like to play golf, but then you feel compelled to go to the club to get your money's worth. Freedom? You buy a cabin at the lake and then drive your family nuts insisting they go to the cabin every weekend. Freedom? You buy season tickets to the basketball game and then have to go to 72 ball games. Freedom? The thing isn't the *thing*. It could be anything. A boat. A car. A trip to the mall. All inherently harmless, except that the enemy often uses these things to invite you to be your own god: "Just take a little bite. Did God *really* mean he didn't want you to have it?"

Maybe we need to rethink how we view freedom. If you want freedom from any item, any emotion, any substance, or any desire, do you normally surround yourself with more of what you are trying to avoid? Usually not. If I'm overweight and I need freedom from sweets, I would not choose to surround myself with an enormous supply of chocolate. So why is it when presented with the concept of financial freedom, one answer is to surround myself with large amounts of money? To have a lot of money may be perceived freedom from want, or from financial fear, but it may not be freedom as money often creates a false security. In my experience, it seems the more money people have, the more time and energy they spend thinking and worrying about it and that attraction can become a barrier to God. That doesn't sound like freedom. As I shared earlier, and it remains true here, whether you have a lot, or a little, it's still not about the money. Freedom is found in the heart.

Jesus tells you to be content: "Let me take care of you. Put your trust in me and not in money or stuff, and I'll give you the desires of your heart." Wanting more is the desire. Taking control is your own declaration of independence. You approach a fork in the road. Will you depend on God or go it alone? It's that simple. This isn't complicated theology. On one path you have what God asks of us, His promises, who He said He is. On the other is, "God, I don't believe you. You take care of the spiritual stuff and let me handle the good stuff." It's a lot like the Parable of the Prodigal Son (See Luke 15:11-32). *I want my inheritance now so I can enjoy life. There are things I want to do; things I want to have.* Notice how many times that first person pronoun "I" appears? The bestselling author and management expert Ken Blanchard describes ego as "edging God out," and that's what happens when we take the wheel. Most of our financial problems begin with "I want," with little or no desire to understand what God wants and end with "I'm sorry."

When you take control, you're jumping into the stream, and off you go with the current. And you know the old saying; even a dead fish can float with the current. You've jumped into the river of the world and will go where the world goes. My dad once said, "If you're driving sixty miles-per-hour on the

> Even a dead fish can float with the current.

highway headed to a destination, don't be surprised that you get there." Every now and then you won't like where you're going and will try to stand against the current. That's your mind fighting against your heart. But eventually, your heart will win, and if your heart is set on being your own master, you will continue to flow with the rest of the world. This is why we see the same money problems affecting Christians that affect non-believers. It's not a question of who you are but *whose* you are. It's not that we're rejecting God or that we quit believing in Him. We still pray, go to church, do all the right things. We even ask him to bless all that we have. But when we insist on calling the financial shots, we miss the true blessings that God desires for us.

FILL IN THE BLANK

Not only do we miss out on God's best for us when we take control of our resources, but we become vulnerable to temptations the enemy dangles in front of us that lead to destruction. It could be an addiction, such as alcohol or gambling. It could be an affair. It could be pornography. Once you become accustomed to having whatever you want whenever you want it, things that were once off limits are now within reach. You listen to the whisper: "God didn't *really* mean you couldn't have (fill in the blank with whatever happens to be the name of your bait)." The reason so many Christians fall victim to ungodly behaviors is that their independence has convinced them they are stronger than they really are. Another word for that is pride. Excess wealth without God's instructions always amplifies existing weaknesses. When the enemy shoots, he aims for the windows of our mind. If he can confuse or distract, it makes his work so much easier.

But even if you are fortunate enough to avoid falling into destructive habits, having your own way leads you further and further from God. Always. You may not realize it at first, but as Jesus warned, "You cannot

> Money makes a lousy savior. It promises much but delivers litte.

serve God and mammon (the Greek word for material wealth)." When you take control rather than submit to God's plan, you have chosen to serve money, things, stuff. And, you know what? Money makes a lousy savior. It promises much but delivers little. I've often said, money can buy happiness, and that's the problem. It can't buy joy. Happiness is fleeting and always demands more. Joy is eternal and transcends wealth (or the lack of wealth). Are you seeing a trend? Whether you may possess a little money or a lot of money, the same factors are at play. A first grader can be preoccupied with a $2 stuffed animal, a high schooler can be distracted with a $25 blouse, a college kid can be distracted by a used car, an adult can be consumed by the next $500 flat-screen TV, a new $30,000 truck, or a $50,000 country club. The money doesn't tell the tale. You must look deeper.

A few years ago, Carrie Underwood captured this truth about taking control with these lyrics to her song, "Jesus Take the Wheel." We can't do it on our own; but the good news is that no matter how far along we are on the path of taking control, we don't have to go back to the fork in the road and start over. God is always right there beside us, patiently inviting us to relinquish the wheel and let Him guide our money matters.

Sometimes in his providence, he uses a strategic interruption to get our attention. It may be a health scare. You could get fired from your job. You might lose your biggest client. On the surface it looks bad, but it gets you to a place where you finally lean into God. More often than not, it's the weight of having to worry about all we have accumulated. The waking up in the middle of the night, worried about your bills, your 401k, the economy, that nagging realization that none of the stuff you have has delivered what you hoped it would and you don't know where to turn.

Eventually, the illusion of control may begin to lose its charm, and that's when you hear it. Not the whisper that beckons you to be your own god, but the still, small voice that says "Trust me."

My friend eventually sold his sailboat. For less than half of what he paid for it. It was an expensive lesson, and one we all have heard but often ignore: Be careful what you ask for because you just might get it.

REFLECTION

CHANGE FOR YOUR DOLLAR

1) When we seek happiness through possessions they tend to possess us instead.
2) The more we fight God for control of our lives, the more control we lose.
3) We often give ourselves the illusion of freedom through the choices we make only to discover we have bound ourselves to difficult situations.
4) Surrendering control is scary, but it is the only way to be truly free.

MONEY IN MOTION

1) Try to identify certain "triggers" that makes you want to accelerate your plans ahead of God's.

2) Name something God has prompted you to journal that may be important for you to share with your spouse.
3) Describe would it look like for you to have "everything you need." And if you had everything you needed, would it *really* be everything?
4) If you are in a position where you have more than you need, think about how you got there and what you should do about it.

PRAYER

You designed me for dependence, and sometimes I act like I want to be on my own, but deep down that's not true. I only want to be on my own as long things are working out the way I want them. As soon as they don't, I want your help and want you in charge again. I know that's not the way it's supposed to be. Lord please let me rest in you and your perfect timing. Amen.

getting what you asked for

The Lord God made garments of skin for Adam and his wife and clothed them. And the Lord God said, "The man has now become like one of us, knowing good and evil. He must not be allowed to reach out his hand and take also from the tree of life and eat, and live forever." So the Lord God banished him from the Garden of Eden to work the ground from which he had been taken. After he drove the man out, he placed on the east side of the Garden of Eden cherubim and a flaming sword flashing back and forth to guard the way to the tree of life.
—Genesis 3:21-24

The metaphorical garden we each lived in when we were just starting out wasn't enough, so we started adding to it, not because we were greedy or materialistic, but because the progression just seemed to make sense. We were making more money, so we could afford a little bigger home in a nicer neighborhood and told ourselves it was a good investment. And it was. A new car was more reliable than a used one, and offered greater resale value. Then we got another promotion, which allowed us to upgrade our furniture. And then we put in a swimming pool because the kids were approaching their teenage years and this would encourage them to have their friends over and stay out of trouble. None of these financial decisions were in essence bad. In fact, at the time they all seemed like the best thing to do. We carefully thought through each of them, shopped for bargain prices, weighed the pros and cons. Anyone on the outside looking in would think we are players in the American success story.

And then the reality set in. It always does. In the sales world, there is an old saying, "Emotion buys it; reality pays for it." Once you decide to take control of your finances, you put yourself in a position to get what you ask for. But as many wiser people have warned, "Be careful what you ask for." Here's the unvarnished truth about possessions: Every little bitty thing we add begins taking up mental and emotional capacity that always has to be resident in your thinking. You can't find rest. In your little "k" kingdom, if you built it, you have to take care of it, you have to protect it, and it always takes away a little piece of yourself. Protecting your kingdom leaves little time or space to enjoy the best from God's Kingdom.

> *Emotion buys it; reality pays for it.*

LITTLE "k" KINGDOMS

I'll never forget how the pride of ownership quickly changed to unrest the first time we sat down for dinner at our brand new dining room table. Anne was setting the table and was about to put a couple of glasses of water on it when I stopped her.

"Whoa! Let me get some coasters first, honey. Those glasses are wet and will leave a mark on our new table."

In fairness to Anne, she was just doing what she always did, but with our old table we didn't care if a glass left a mark or not. The table already had its share of nicks and blemishes. Sort of gave it character. And, I'm not really a neat freak and probably contributed my share of stains on our old table. But all of a sudden, I worried about this new table because I knew how much it cost. Instead of just sitting down as I always had and enjoying a meal with my wife, I became anxious as I was using this object for its intended purpose. The function of the table hadn't changed. It did its job no better or worse than our old table. But I changed. I now had to think about it. Protect it. And with each additional purchase, the same thing happened. More hooks + more distractions = less God.

Now don't get me wrong. Taking care of what we own is a good thing. It would be poor stewardship not to treat things properly. It would be irresponsible (and could lead to costly repairs) if you never had the oil changed in your car or spilled coffee on your computer keyboard or dropped

> *More hooks + more distractions = less God.*

your cell phone in the toilet (not that it's ever happened to me). It's just that the more stuff we accumulate, the more prominence it has in our lives. We never start out with the intention of becoming slaves to our possessions. Yet, with each purchase we gradually move from owner to owned. In contrast, Jesus urges us to adopt a more carefree attitude about our possessions:

> *Therefore I tell you, do not worry about your life, what you will eat or drink; or about your body, what you will wear. Is not life more than food, and the body more than clothes? Can any one of you by worrying add a single hour to your life?*
>
> —Matthew 6:25, 27

But worry we do. Beware the noisy whisper of all our stuff screaming for attention. It can drown out the voice of God who wants us to use His provision to serve Him and serve others. Even if we heard His voice, we may not recognize its relevance because now, in our own little "k" kingdoms, we're too busy maintaining the barriers we've built. We work at stressful jobs and come home only to face more work in tending to all

> *Big trucks with big trailers don't make sharp turns.*

our stuff. So often I have found Christian families whose lives were full, but not fulfilling. There's no margin—nothing left for taking care of those things God wants us to do. There is no room left to be dependent on Him and to live for others. Let me put it another way. Big trucks with big trailers don't make sharp turns. How long would it take you to turn if God asked you to? Are you a reasonable size, sure-footed, and nimble enough to change directions if you heard God inviting you to something different, more exciting, more fulfilling?

We took control because we thought we knew what we wanted. We thought that having what we wanted would make us happy. For a brief period it does. They really do. I love that new car smell and those first few trips in it. But after a while, the shine wears off and it's just a car. Anne loves putting on a new outfit—and I love

> *You can have God, and you can have stuff, but you cannot love them both.*

the way she looks in it. But after a few times wearing it, it's just clothing. Jesus warns us that cars rust and clothes attract moths (Matthew 6:20). Later in that passage he counsels us that our hearts follow whatever we treasure. Let that sink in: our hearts follow what we treasure.

Eventually the stuff we believe we cannot live without requires more from us than it delivers. It's not only that it doesn't deliver, but that it sucks the life out of us as we try to protect it. By the way, I'm not talking about reckless purchases or compulsive shoppers. That's a whole 'nuther story. What I'm referring to happens to intelligent, serious-minded, responsible Christians who would consider themselves to be very careful about their spending. The problem isn't so much with the spending but with the plan. Man's plan is to get what he wants; God's plan is to give where the needs are great. You can have God and you can have stuff, but you cannot love them both.

Over the years I have known many people who bought vacation homes and things didn't turn out quite like they planned and their stories had similar themes. A gentleman was blessed with a high-paying, though stressful, job. He decided he wanted a vacation place to use and relax with his family. In his mind, this would not be an extravagant purchase, but an inexpensive way for his family to enjoy some quality time together. You might wonder, *How can a vacation home be inexpensive?* The plan was to buy the house with a low down payment and then rent it out for all but two weeks a year when he and his family would enjoy the house. On paper, it was a great plan as these things often are. Purchasing the house could be a wise investment. The rental payments would cover the mortgage and in twenty years or so the house would be completely paid off and he could sell it at a profit or live there.

But everything didn't go okay. An unexpected financial downturn came at the wrong time and what they had bought for a lot of money, they couldn't sell for as much. Then, the rental income he had planned on using to pay the mortgage on the house was much less than what he was expecting and the upkeep and expenses still had to be paid.

So now he was feeling overextended mentally and emotionally. Fortunately, he had the money to ride out the storm for a bit, but that couldn't last. The distraction and stress of owning this vacation home created a lot of unwelcome noise in an already fully-saturated life. On top of

> *When we work off of our plan and get what we want, rarely does it turn out the way we imagined.*

everything, this house was becoming a wedge between him and his wife. This was not the way it was planned. What was expected to bring joy was now bringing concern and complexity. We've all heard it before, "I thought it would be different." When we work off of our plan and get what we want, rarely does it turn out the way *we* imagined.

After thinking about it he knew exactly what he needed to do. It was a mental and emotional drain. He needed to sell it, but it would be at a significant loss. It would take courage.

Owning the house and pouring even more money into it was no longer worth the added financial pressure and the headaches in his marriage. If you're flying a plane and you need to jettison some cargo or crash, I don't care what the cargo is—as long as it's not someone—get rid of it! That's what he did.

How could this really smart guy get himself into such a distressing situation? He took a risk and it didn't work out. It happens every day. Other times, we take risks

> *Just because you can pay for it, doesn't mean you can afford it.*

and it works out just the way *we* planned. Unfortunately, you never know the outcome ahead of time.

God warns us not to presume on the future as a basis for our decisions today (see James 4:13). This man also found himself emotionally overextended and consumed by the very things he wanted. Often, we make affordability a primary criteria for our financial decisions. There is a lesson that bears to repeated again. Just because you can pay for it, doesn't mean you can afford it.

BANKING ON THE FUTURE

Add to that the presumption that the future will look as good or better than today, and you get another dangerous duo: "I can afford it and I think everything is going to be okay."

Remember that house I just had to have but knew I couldn't afford? As soon as the contractor put together a deal that made the monthly payments affordable, it was mine. Those "affordable" purchases often come back to haunt us because we presume upon the future. As long as my income stayed the same, that house that was just barely out of my reach would be affordable. As long as the economy kept rumbling along, owning that vacation home made sense.

This may sound like a quote from Captain Obvious, but what may not be so obvious to many of us is this: When we place our complete trust in God we can be certain that His plan for us will be better than our own plans. *"For I know the plans I have for you,"* declares the Lord, *"plans to prosper you and not to harm you, plans to give you a hope and a future"* (Jeremiah 29:11).

> *When we place our complete trust in God we can be certain that His plan for us will be better than our own plans.*

It goes back to the whisper in the garden—lies that sound so true. Think for a moment about that fantasy item you'd really like to have. It can be anything, big or small. New cell phone or latest tablet? Mountain biking trip to the Rockies? A hybrid car? A house renovation? A man-cave? Initially, it may seem frivolous, unnecessary, or out of your price range. It doesn't make a lot of sense, but it's fun to think about.

That's when it happens. What began as a glance has become a gaze. It's too late. Your "wanter" has been switched on and is locked on a target. The inner-workings of your financial choices start churning and begin to piece together your case of justification to acquire the new item.

As you keep thinking about it, you start to hear the whisper: *It's not that expensive. You can afford it. It's on sale and will never be cheaper. Besides, it will make you happier. You're going to enjoy it for years to come. It will bring you closer together.* It doesn't have to be true; it just has to appear to be true. This is the enemy at his finest and you are very close to getting what you wanted.

Seriously? Can you think of a single purchase that has brought you closer to your spouse? Are you still experiencing happiness from the (*fill in the blank*) you purchased five years ago? In most cases, when we get that wonderful thing that we wanted so badly, from that moment on we start worrying about losing it. Most things with a price tag have hooks in them that grab hold of us and never let go. They may be just

> *It doesn't have to be true; it just has to appear to be true.*

things but we invest them with such importance that they end up becoming matters of the heart. They are no longer things; they have developed a life of their own, one that demands our full allegiance. None of us will ever say it, but getting what we want is based on the belief that happiness, joy, fulfillment, and meaning come from some place other than God. It's like the old Burger King jingle, "Have it your way"—you may be able to afford what you want, but is it really good for you?

> *"I have the right to do anything," you say—but*
> *not everything is beneficial.*
> —1 Corinthians 6:12

God invites us to trust Him, focus on others rather than on ourselves and be the salt and light that the world desperately needs. And while we agree with all of that, we want something more. We want God to be alongside us, but we still want what we want. We want His plan as well as our own, and that's where the confusion comes in. We convince ourselves that they're the same. We take the truth—God loves you and has a plan for you—and bend it ever so slightly. I'm prospering, so I must be following God's plan. He wouldn't have given me so much provision without expecting me to enjoy some of it. How can a statement be so true and so false at the same time?

> *Most of us are experts at turning our personal desires into God's "bountiful blessings."*

But it doesn't work that way. Ever. As long as I want *this* more than that, I'll always choose *this*. I don't doubt that you want God to be an integral part of your life, but if you want something else more than you want God, guess what? That's exactly what you will get. Unfortunately, the price we pay is only an entry fee into the race of wanting more.

Most of us are experts at turning our personal desires into God's "bountiful blessings."

It's important to note that getting what you want—and the dangers that come with it—is not about wealth or riches. Rich or poor, when we place our trust in things, we are never satisfied. The great Russian novelist Fyodor Dostoyevsky expertly describes this dilemma in a passage from *The Brothers Karamazov*:

> *The world says: "You have needs—satisfy them. You have as much right as the rich and the mighty. Don't hesitate to satisfy your needs; indeed, expand your needs and demand more." This is the worldly doctrine of today. And they believe that this is freedom. The result for the rich is isolation and suicide, for the poor, envy and murder."*

That was written in 1880. Have things changed much? So is it wrong to get what you want? Not at all. I believe God really does want us to enjoy nice things, as long as we hold onto them loosely so they don't distract us from Him or His plans for us. Remember the passage about worry from Jesus' Sermon on the Mount I quoted earlier? Later in that sermon Jesus offers a hint about how to avoid the pitfalls of getting what we want: *"But seek first His [God's] kingdom and His righteousness, and all these things will be given to you as well"* (Matthew 6:33). If your priority is obeying God, your possessions will not own you. But how do you accomplish that? How do you own something without it owning you?

If you find yourself worrying about your stuff, you may want to get rid of that stuff.

You start by paying attention to the things you do during the day that keep you up at night. If you're constantly worrying about your tennis game, tennis may be more important to you than it should be. Scale back, get it into perspective, or you may need to quit playing if it becomes too much of a barrier. It's that simple. Remember, Jesus said that worry adds nothing to your life (see

Matthew 6:27). If you find yourself worrying about your stuff, you may want to get rid of that stuff. Now you may say, "John, that's pretty drastic!" I understand it may sound that way, and it may be drastic. But how long do you wait to take action? I'm not talking about the occasional concern or burden about a financial choice that can be opened up, reviewed, and resolved. I'm talking about the chronic worry that stems from poor past choices, our unhealthy attractions to things we have, and/or fears of the future.

A number of times I have come across the rare family who has fought the good fight, trusted in the promises of God, and got a lot of this right. I've seen it personally and I've heard about it. I'm not talking about perfection; I'm talking about faithful progress. Such is one story of a very good friend whose thriving business made him wealthy. He loves the outdoors so he bought a lovely home on about forty acres graced with a couple of ponds. He put in trails and a swimming dock and had the house beautifully appointed with tasteful furniture, including lovely artwork on the walls. It's a gorgeous setting—the minute you step onto the property your cares just melt away in the peaceful beauty.

For years, he and his adult children and his grandkids have gathered for wonderful times of family fun and worship there. They swim, fish, hike the trails, sit around a big round table for meals, (and yes, you have to use coasters or Gramma won't be happy). There are plenty of toys for everyone, and a big front porch for watching the sun set over the big pond at the end of the day.

He is successful from the world's perspective. Through God's provision, he has all he could want. But there's more to the story. What he really wanted, and what he has achieved is not simply a getaway for him and his family. Except for the few weeks that his family is there, this gorgeous property becomes a refuge for people in ministry and those in need of solitude for refreshment and healing. People enjoy this property who could never afford a place like this. He hands them the keys and it's theirs. No strings attached. He doesn't charge them a penny. He just wants them to have the same opportunity he does to enjoy the beauty, relax, recharge, and feel the presence of the Holy Spirit. I don't have the exact numbers, but my guess is that he and his family enjoy this wonderful property about ten or twenty percent of the year—the remaining time it's handed over to others and it ministers to them in the name of Christ. Christian music you have probably heard has been recorded there, marriages have been saved, youth have found Christ, groups have journeyed, and most recently I sat in its solitude and felt God's presence as I worked on this book.

Now trust me, this place needs to be maintained. Stuff breaks and has to be repaired. Some of the guests include youth groups who spill things and make messes to be cleaned up. But my friend doesn't seem to lose any sleep over those things, and that's because sharing this second home with others brings him more joy than if he were to use it only for himself. Far from perfect, but he seems to have done a pretty good job navigating the waters of God's provision, his own financial choices and opportunities.

So how do you get a handle on all the variables that affect your financial choices? Let's look to a model from the cross that illustrates primary areas that affect our financial choices—The Cross Paradigm.

Let me first describe the paradigm. At the top and base of the cross, we have two competing perspectives—"God's Plan" and "My Plan." (I'll let you guess which one is usually better!) At the right and left of the paradigm, we have our first two silent partners. On the right is "Worry & Want," that lives in the future, and on the left is "Shame & Regret," that lives in our past. Our other two silent partners rest beneath "My Plan" perspective and these are "Beliefs & Behaviors." Finally, in the center, living between your past and your future, is the only area of your life that you can affect. This is your "Now" and with you today is the team of "Faith & Love" that is only found in Christ and they are ready to follow Him. Are you ready?

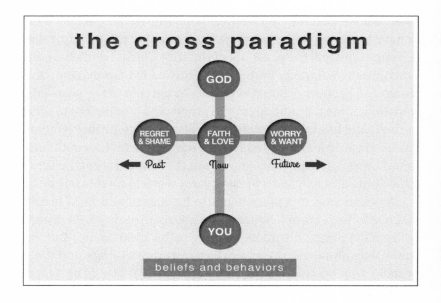

As a follower of Christ, it is likely that all of these paradigm characteristics affect your financial choices in one way or another. If you're like me, when a financial choice is presented, my first thought is usually, *How does it affect me?* Then the silent partners kick in. What do I *believe* about that? Everything you've heard, read, seen, etc. goes into this question. Next, certain *behaviors* begin on autopilot, without you even knowing it. Then finally I might get around to thinking a little of God's perspective after I've gone through all the other perspectives. How backward is that? My personal prayer is that I begin to think about my financial choices from His perspective first, far before my personal desires crank up. I'm getting better, but far from where I want to be. Progress, not perfection is our objective.

Now, if only one or two of these silent partners were involved, it would be confusing enough, but what if all of them were active at the same time?! It's easy to see how our financial choices can become so confusing and off track leading to results that are equally disruptive. To add even more complexity, if only one person was dealing with these silent partners around their financial choices, it would be challenging enough. But when you add a man and a woman, in marriage, they each bring their own paradigms to the relationship. In the illustration below we see how these complexities are doubled!

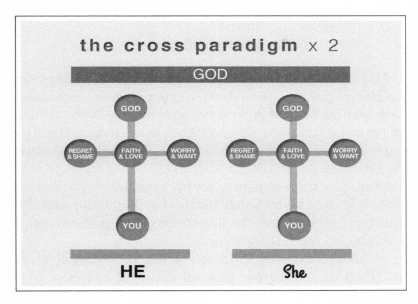

Couples each bring different spiritual maturities and views of who God is. They also bring their own versions of the silent partners. This can create an underlying confusion that usually goes unnoticed for years, if it is ever noticed at all. Differences in opinion can result. Disagreements stem from the differences. One argument leads to another and we begin to protect ourselves and stay away from these marital and financial land mines. These can sit quietly for years, creating an underlying tension and unhealthiness to the strongest marriages. They aren't necessarily fatal, but they are thieves of our unity and joy. It's common for a man and a woman to approach each money moment from their own unique perspective.

- He perceives, she perceives,
- He regrets, she regrets,
- He wants, she wants,
- He believes, she believes,
- He behaves, she behaves,
- He chooses, she chooses,
- Then . . . **He Spends, She Spends.**

As you see, couples each have different past choices and experiences that have created their current situations. In addition, these past choices and experiences have trained each of them in unique ways that in turn will affect their choices today and into the future. She is fearful of certain situations, he is fearful of others. The list continues . . .

I hope you are beginning to see the variables that impact our financial choices. It's no wonder finances rank at the top of the list of marital problems, and the fallout from those problems sends shockwaves through our families.

We all have experienced "Shame & Regret," "Worry & Want," and "Faith & Love" in our financial decisions, and most of us understand how our beliefs influence all we do, including our money choices. What I've found over the years is that very few families understand their own behaviors that occur without a full appreciation of their power or effect. Even though these terms may be new to you, these behaviors have been affecting people like you and me for thousands of years, around much more than their money. Let me share some financial behavior basics[1] and some corresponding biblical examples:

Mental Accounting – People tend to think that not all money is created equally. I think this is the most common misbehavior of all. You can earn money, find money, receive it as a gift, get a bonus at work, or possibly get a tax refund. Interestingly, most people think about each of these money sources very differently. For example, if you found a $20 bill and you could not locate the owner, most people tend to spend it on themselves, very few add it to their budget. A tax refund can turn into a windfall that is spent unwisely. Here's the point. As God is provision, our money can come from different sources, yet it is all from Him to be used for His glory.

> **A Lot or a Little?** - *And He looked up and saw the rich putting their gifts into the treasury, and He saw also a certain poor widow putting in two mites. So He said, "Truly I say to you that this poor widow has put in more than all; for all these out of their abundance have put in offerings for God, but she out of her poverty put in all the livelihood that she had."*
>
> —Luke 21:1-4

Framing – Decisions are made based on how choices are presented. I'll sometimes ask a friend if they would be able to give away 20% of their income? Most say "no." I will then ask the same person if they could live on 80% of their income if they had to? Most say "yes." So, then I'll ask, "What's the difference?" There is none. Pay attention to the way financial questions are posed, or, how you pose them to yourself. The same question can be asked in different ways and get very different answers. Always compare your "answers" to God's truth and you will always answer wisely regardless of the question.

> **Did God Really Say . . .** - *Now the serpent was more crafty than any of the wild animals the LORD God had made. He said to the woman, "Did God really say, 'You must not eat from any tree in the garden'?"*
>
> —Genesis 3:1

Status Quo Bias – People tend to "follow the herd" even when it is not in their best interest. Can everyone else be wrong and you are the only who is right? You better believe it. However, many of us let "the crowd" override what we sense to be true and we lose our confidence in the midst of their movement. If the crowd moves, only follow if they are headed toward Christ, otherwise, stand your ground. You'll be glad you did.

> ***Golden Peer Pressure*** *- When the people saw that Moses was so long in coming down from the mountain, they gathered around Aaron and said, "Come, make us gods who will go before us. As for this fellow Moses who brought us up out of Egypt, we don't know what has happened to him." Aaron answered them, "Take off the gold earrings that your wives, your sons and your daughters are wearing, and bring them to me." So all the people took off their earrings and brought them to Aaron. He took what they handed him and made it into an idol cast in the shape of a calf, fashioning it with a tool. Then they said, "These are your gods, Israel, who brought you up out of Egypt."*
>
> —Exodus 32: 1-4

Decision Paralysis – The more choices and barriers people face, the more likely they are to do nothing. Have you ever noticed this? If you have only one or two items to choose from, it may be difficult, but you can probably make your choice. If you had eight or ten options to choose from, it could be overwhelming and many times, no choice is made. The result is that you can remain in a state of confusion and stress. Unfortunately, not to choose is to choose.

> ***Scared Stiff*** *- Then the man who had received one bag of gold came. "Master," he said, "I knew that you are a hard man, harvesting where you have not sown and gathering where you have not scattered seed. So I was afraid and went out and hid your gold in the ground. See, here is what belongs to you."*
>
> —Matthew 25:24-25

Overconfidence – People tend to overestimate their own abilities, knowledge, and skills, and are overly optimistic about their financial futures. So often people want to handle their finances on their own. I admire do-it-yourselfers as long as they have all the resources needed. To DIY with your finances, you need TDK. You need the TIME, you need the DESIRE to want to do it, and, you need the KNOWLEDGE, both financial and scriptural. If you don't have all three, don't try to DIY.

> *A Foolish Farmer* - *Then he said, 'This is what I'll do. I will tear down my barns and build bigger ones, and there I will store my surplus grain. And I'll say to myself, 'You have plenty of grain laid up for many years. Take life easy; eat, drink and be merry.'"*
> —Luke 12:18-19

Our silent partners are very real and can wreak havoc on our financial lives, which in turn can wreak havoc on our personal lives, our faith, our vocations, and our relationships. The first step is knowing that they exist. The second step is watching for them in your choices.

Whether you have more than you need or less than you need, we all have a desire for certain financial goals and there are a lot of variables that impact that desire. We will make financial mistakes and sometimes get caught up in chasing the world. Reaching your financial goals only works if they include being obedient to Christ—a truth best experienced in the company of others.

I hope as we understand and take control of the paradigms around our money choices, that we will grow in our faith, make better financial choices, and free up even more generous resources to spread the good news of Jesus Christ.

REFLECTION

CHANGE FOR YOUR DOLLAR

1) It's easy to get caught up in the emotion surrounding and driving your spending and forget the realities of the costs involved.

2) Too often the things we acquire that we expect to make life better end up complicating it instead.

3) When we bank on the future without any preparation for today, we end up creating regrets that follow us.

4) Shifting your thinking so your first consideration is God's perspective removes barriers of worry & want, regret & shame, and allows you to choose from a place of faith & love, a place called today.

5) Our personal experiences, training, and educations create in each of us a unique approach to financial decisions that automatically affects your choices.

MONEY IN MOTION

1) Think about what you get from your money and stuff (comfort, security, etc.) that God wants you to get from Him.

2) Try to recall the best financial advice you ever received and see if you can find its biblical basis.

3) Name a purchase where you and your spouse did not agree. Describe how it made each of you feel both before and after the purchase, and the outcome.

4) If you tend to "keep score" of purchases—*he spends* $50, *then she spends* $50—think of ways this practice could a) bring you closer, or b) drive wedge between you.

PRAYER

Lord, I thought it would be different than this. I thought I could handle the balancing act of my plans and your plans. From the outside I may appear successful in many ways, yet what really matters has been steadily fading away. I know it and you know it. Help me want you more than I want these worldly ways. Let my life reflect you. I pray that you would lead me to your path back to you. Amen.

we're not alone

The Lord foils the plans of the nations; He thwarts the purposes of the peoples. But the plans of the Lord stand firm forever, the purposes of His heart through all generations. Blessed is the nation whose God is the Lord, the people He chose for His inheritance. From heaven the Lord looks down and sees all mankind; from His dwelling place he watches all who live on earth—He who forms the hearts of all, who considers everything they do.
—Genesis 3:21-24

Imagine yourself sitting in church on Sunday morning. The worship leader invites everyone to stand as the praise band opens with a familiar chorus that normally lifts your heart and soul. But not this Sunday. You've just got too much rattling around in your brain. You try to get into the flow of the worship; you want to experience the joy that everyone else seems to have, but inside you're a wreck. Everything seems to be coming due at the same time: the car payment, the mortgage, the fees on your son's college applications. Normally these things would not be a big deal, but your boss announced that there would be no bonuses this year. And, at least on paper, you lost a bundle on a deal your broker said was a no-brainer. Now *you're* feeling like the no-brainer!

You look to your left and there's Mike and Cindy, faces all aglow, arms raised, singing for all they're worth. You look to your right, and you see the same from Rich and Denise. In fact, everyone around you seems to be caught up in the power of the moment, recharging their spiritual batteries for the week ahead. But your battery is running low. Your battery needs more than a jumpstart, it needs to be replaced.

It's very likely Mike and Cindy may be struggling with the same financial issues you are. Ditto for Rich and Denise. From my experience, all Christian couples wrestle with financial issues. And I believe that will always be true as long as anyone handles money. We should expect struggles when using the currency of a temporal world for the plans of an eternal Kingdom. The point here is not the financial issues but where our hearts and minds gravitate in the midst of them. God did not promise a lack of struggles, just

> *We should expect struggles when using the currency of a temporal world for the plans of an eternal Kingdom.*

that He would be there beside us to guide us as we face them. You can set your mind and your heart in the perfect confidence that God and His plans are there for you, they will never fail and they have never changed.

> *The counsel of the Lord stands forever, the plans of*
> *His heart to all generations.*
> —Psalm 33:11

One of the sinister forces that keep us trapped in the snares of the money myth is that we think we're the only ones who have ever screwed up our finances. Money is one of those things we don't like to talk about, especially if we're having problems with it. When things are going well financially, we don't want to say too much because it might seem as if we're bragging. So we offer righteous-sounding hints about our affluence like, "We're truly blessed," or "God has been good to us." The pursuit of abundant riches can be a common sin that gets a wink and a smile.

NO ONE WANTS TO TALK ABOUT IT

When things aren't going so well, we change the subject if it veers to the topic of money while there are some good reasons to not open up your bank accounts for everyone to see, the downside of our reticence is that we start thinking we're the only ones in trouble. We feel isolated in our frustration over money and things to inhibit our heart's desire to love and serve God more fully.

Many, if not most, of those surrounding us in church on that Sunday morning are likely wrestling with financial hardships; they just might be a little better at hiding their pain.

Some of us are dealing with the distraction of abundance; others are dealing with distraction of scarcity.

In other words, we're not alone. When it comes to spending more but enjoying it less, you're in good company, including yours truly. I've made every bad financial decision in the book, but have lived to tell about it.

According to John W. Kennedy in *Christianity Today*, "remarkably, American consumers are simultaneously earning record income while accumulating record debt. And there is little difference between the amounts that Christians and non-Christians earn, spend, save, charge, or donate to charities."[2] From the Federal Reserve, we learn that the tab for our debt comes to nearly $2.4 trillion. That works out to be nearly $7,800 in debt per person in the U.S. Of course, unless you think the nation's five-year-olds have run up huge debts at Toys R Us, the number is higher when isolated to adults.

> *Some of us are dealing with the distraction of abundance, others are dealing with distraction of scarcity.*

A lot of that debt comes from the ease of obtaining and using credit cards or one-click ordering on your smart phone. See something you like, but no cash in the wallet? No problem. Swipe a plastic card or tap your phone and it's yours. According to information gathered by the U.S. Census Bureau, 181 million Americans possess approximately 1.5 billion credit cards, or nearly nine cards per owner.[3]

Instead of "what have you got in *your* wallet," the commercial should ask, "how *many* do you have in your wallet?" And why? Some people who have more than one credit card are playing the, "Which one won't get rejected because it's over the credit limit" lottery." We learn early that all it takes is a little piece of plastic to get what you want. Remember that first day away at college where you got a free T-shirt or some other gift if you signed up for a Visa card? Have you been enticed by the promise of points toward airline miles for an upgrade to First Class? I'm going to let you in on a secret. It is usually cheaper, clearer, and much less risky, to pay cash.

The good news is your situation does not have to be a terminal condition. Lots of people in the Bible made the same choices

> *We learn early that all it takes is a little piece of plastic to get what you want.*

you've made and lived to tell about it, though they didn't live a joyful life. When the rich young ruler could not follow Jesus' command to sell all he had and give to the poor, he walked away sadly (see Matthew 19:22). He probably continued to live his royal life but most likely remained in a state of regret. Others, such as Judas, even though they tried to hide their avarice, their love for money and their unguarded hearts led to their ultimate downfall and destruction (see Matthew 26:15).

It's also easy to look back on the good old days of our parents and grandparents and think they were too wise to be fooled by this mirage, but they made their share of mistakes too. People don't like to talk about things like original sin, but ever since Adam and Eve got what they wanted, we've been cursed with the same desire. If trusting money and things instead of God weren't universal temptations, the Bible wouldn't have so much to say about it.

According to many sources, the Bible has more than 2,000 verses concerning money and possessions, including:

- Do not wear yourself out to get rich; have the wisdom to show restraint. (Proverbs 23:4)
- Wealth is worthless in the day of wrath, but righteousness delivers from death. (Proverbs 11: 4)
- You cannot serve both God and money." (Matthew 6:24)

God knew the power of the enemy's whisper to gradually pull us away from Him. His warnings against wealth were not to prevent us from earning money or even enjoying it, but to prevent us from being caught in its grasp. Remember, what He wants more than anything

If trusting money and things instead of God weren't universal temptations, the Bible wouldn't have so much to say about it.

is to have a relationship with you, and that's difficult if you are wrapped up in obtaining and maintaining.

You are not the first person who truly loves God to believe the lie that a little more money would make you happier and more content. And you won't be the last. Most of your friends have made the same choices you have made. The fact that you're still alive, sitting in church, driving home from work, or waking up in worry in the middle of the night says you still have a chance to resolve this.

The enemy wants you to believe it's too late, but once again, that's a lie. There's always hope when you follow Christ. I will never understand God's timing, but I know it's always perfect. For some reason God may have chosen now to enlighten you to the fact that you have choices. I've heard it said many times that if it wasn't for the valleys, the mountains wouldn't seem so tall. If you need shade, the best time to plant an oak tree was thirty years ago. But the next best time to plant an oak tree is today.

Now is the perfect time for us each to draw closer to God, begin giving up control, and live the way he intended. We can do this together, the way God planned.

THE SEVEN

You may have gotten into a financial mess because you wanted to be completely in control, or maybe you made a poor choice, or fell into a trap of the enemy. Perhaps you have experienced a financial hazard that was not of your own doing. Regardless of the source or the extent of your financial pain, you can begin the healing process by turning to the many wonderful resources God has given you. I like to call them *The Seven* and they are the keys to enjoying His provision rather than losing sleep over your money issues. Think of *The Seven* as your own unique set of counsel and advice—waiting to help you, ready to support you and prepared to help you fight.

> *For lack of guidance a nation falls,*
> *but victory is won through many advisers.*
> —Proverbs 11:14

None of these by themselves will prevent the enemy from whispering to you, nor will they automatically keep you from making a poor choice. *The Seven* can give you the wisdom and motivation to ignore and fight the enemy, thwart him, silence him, and make prayerfully better choices. Spiritual battles are fought with spiritual weapons on spiritual battlefields.

> *Therefore put on the full armor of God, so that when the*
> *day of evil comes, you may be able to stand your ground,*
> *and after you have done everything, to stand. 14 Stand*
> *firm then, with the belt of truth buckled around your*
> *waist, with the breastplate of righteousness in place,*
> *and with your feet fitted with the readiness that comes*

from the gospel of peace. In addition to all this, take up the shield of faith, with which you can extinguish all the flaming arrows of the evil one. Take the helmet of salvation and the sword of the Spirit, which is the word of God.

—Ephesians 6:13-17

As I described with the Cross Paradigm, up until now, fear and worry of the future, regrets, and shame from the past, your beliefs and behaviors, and actions of today, sit at your planning table. Let *The Seven* create peace, rest and space today to get rid of those concerns and make room for God's work and plans to flourish in your lives.

#1 - PRAYER

According to Oswald Chambers, "prayer does not equip us for greater works; prayer is the greater work." I know. Almost too simple and predictable, so let me frame it this way: When was the last time you prayed about a purchase? If we pray at all about our finances, it's usually a last-minute, panicked cry for help: "Lord, fix this mess and get me out of debt!" But before you bought that GoPro, did you pray about it? What about the vacation to Myrtle Beach? The addition to your home? These seem so mundane— why bother God about them? What does He care whether I buy a Corolla or a Tesla? According to the Bible, He doesn't care that much about the camera, the car, or the vacation, but He cares a lot about you. *"Cast all your anxiety on him because he cares for you."* (1 Peter 5:7 NLT). He wants you to be free from the burden of what often accompanies the accumulation of stuff so He can enjoy an unencumbered relationship with you.

Prayer undergirds our walk with Christ. Prayer aligns our hearts and minds with God. What I have learned—and am still learning—is that the act of seeking God's guidance through prayer causes me to slow down and think more clearly about a financial decision. Do I hear some big voice saying, "buy" or "don't buy?" Not yet, but always, prayer always opens my eyes to what is important to God. Then it's up to me to decide if I want Him and His plans more than I want the stuff. God's guidance becomes clear through prayer; the struggle comes in whether or not we follow it.

Obviously, God wants us to come to Him with our urgent needs as well, so if you're bottoming out financially the best place to start your recovery is on your knees. Just don't stop there. Try this experiment: for the next week, pray about everything that involves spending money—from a trip to McDonald's to moving money around in your investments. If you are diligent, you will sense God's direction and will want to make this a permanent habit.

#2 - GOD'S WORD

Full disclosure: I believe the Bible is true, trustworthy, and relevant. In fact, anything in this book that seems wise or prudent comes directly from God's word. If you read something you like in this book, thank God. If you read something that you don't like, that's me! The Bible's guidance on how to live is the most reliable resource for anyone who wants to live a godly life. And when it comes to money, wealth, and possessions, the Bible has plenty to say, mostly along the lines of "be careful."

A lot of Christians try to read the Bible regularly, but often fail to do so on a consistent basis. According to the Center for Bible Engagement, only about fourteen percent of Americans read their Bibles on most days of the week.[4] Since approximately seventy-six percent of Americans are Christians that means very few of us read our Bibles regularly. In the most recent Barna research for the American Bible Society's State of the Bible 2015 study, sixty percent of Americans want to read the Bible more. However, forty-two percent of respondents share that being too busy with life's responsibilities is the number one reason for their decrease in Bible engagement. And thirty-three percent of U.S. adults identify not having enough time to read their Bible as their top frustration. In my own experience, when I'm all wrapped up in my money issues—distracted and struggling with more going out than is coming in—I'm less likely to spend time in the Word, yet that's when we need it most. In our financial lives we should always retain a posture where more income is coming in than expenses going out. Interestingly, prayer is the exact opposite; the more prayer we get going out, the more God shows up in our lives. It's been said you can't out-give God, but you can't out-pray Him either! How cool is that?

> *Consistently spending time in God's word helps innoculate us from the false truth that happiness comes from more money and things.*

Consistently spending time in God's Word helps inoculate us from the false truth that happiness comes from more money and things. There's no magic formula for reading the Bible regularly, but a number of fine organizations have produced easy-to-use plans that will get you through the entire Bible in a year. (See bible reading resources on the FREE page at JohnHPutnam.com.)

If you don't read the Bible regularly, you could start any time. According to the results from the American Bible Society 2015 study by Barna, engaged Bible readers (those reading the Bible 3-4 times per week) is on the decline. From my perspective, this is happening at the same time that financial burdens and concerns are growing for many Christians. Even though I don't have any formal data to support this claim, there is no question these two are related somehow.

And when you begin reading God's word regularly, if you miss a day, give yourself the gift of grace and get back at it tomorrow. And pay attention to what you're reading. Ask yourself, what is God trying to tell me with this passage? What nugget of truth have I read that I can use in my day-to-day decisions? I'm not a big journaler, but I do keep a small notebook and pen beside me when I read the Bible. God just seems to speak to me in those moments and brings things to mind that I need to wrestle with in front of Him. Be expectant for His voice and be bold with what he shares.

#3 - YOUR SPOUSE

I'd be willing to bet that in most Christian families, the guy handles all the money stuff and pretty much keeps things close to the vest—not out of any sinister motives or desire to hide things. Even if both spouses have successful careers, it's just the way things generally work out. Now that's not every couple, as I know many women who are gifted financial thinkers and take the helm for the family, but after twenty-five years working with families, I've found it is the exception. So many times I have seen wives defer their input and interest as long as they believe they are "okay." When any wife or husband defers their financial responsibility to their spouse, it is a problem waiting to happen.

In business enterprise, financial decisions are usually brought before a team. The CFO or CEO may have the final authority on how money is spent and used, but I don't know of a single person at that level who would make a decision without getting input from others. Yet, in our marriages, we often go it alone. Or if we check with our spouses, it's often just a way to justify our decisions rather than to solicit advice. It usually goes something like this:

> He: "Honey, we could save a lot of money on our family vacations if we bought an RV, so why don't you come with me Saturday and help me pick one out?"

> She: "Wow! They're pretty expensive? Are you sure we can afford it?"

He: "Great question, but I've run the numbers and based on our previous vacations, the RV will pay for itself in five years."

She: "Well, it does sound like a lot of fun, but we've never done anything like that."

He: "That's what's so great about it—we'll learn as we go—it will be an adventure."

He would probably tell all of us that he always consults with his spouse before any major purchase. But what he really means is that he runs it by her and then goes ahead with what he wants. I don't know how many times I've heard one spouse or the other remark that they were not really all-in on a deal but never actually had the opportunity to talk it through with their spouse. In some cases, failure to involve a spouse in financial decisions drives a wedge in the relationship that creates unnecessary tension. Money issues are consistently at the top of the lists of reasons why marriages fail. Cross-training on paying bills, dealing with accounts, meeting together with advisors, and other personal financial activities are a must!

> *Money issues are consistently at the top of the lists of reasons why marriages fail.*

At the risk of causing your spouse to faint, ask for his or her input with every check you write or card you swipe for the next month. Begin to think of that person as your business partner. Set aside time each week or month to go over your online banking or family budget. For one of you, this will feel like a loss of control and you know what—it is. If you find yourself struggling with this, re-read Chapter V to get on track and stay there. In fact, your marriage *and* your finances will be better.

#4 - CLOSE FRIEND

If you're fortunate, you will have two or three really close friends with whom you can share just about anything. If you're really fortunate, at least one of those friends loves God more than he or she loves you and will tell you the truth even if it makes you mad.

I once heard my friend, Kem Wilson, put it in perfect terms. "We all need a truth-teller in our lives. A truth-teller is someone who loves Jesus more than they love you." I don't know if that

> *A truth-teller is someone who loves Jesus more than they love you.*

was Kem's quote or whether he was sharing a pearl of someone else's wisdom, but I immediately went out and found someone who would be a truth-teller for me, and I would wholeheartedly recommend you to do the same. That person needs to be on your "team," and before you make any major financial decision, you need to get his or her input. I didn't say you need their permission—you want their input. What you do with what God gives you is always your sole responsibility.

Here's where knowing who your friends are is important. When I was in my "bigger, better, stronger, faster" phase, (better known as the "Steve Austin years" of course referring to the "The Six Million Dollar Man") I had a lot of "friends" who encouraged me to go for it. Like the guy who said, "Nobody successful lives there," or the builder who thought he was helping me when he greased the wheels on an "affordable" mortgage payment. If I mentioned to a buddy at church that we were thinking about buying a new house, the response was always, "That's great, John!" These weren't bad people, and I'm sure they meant well. But what I really needed was a guy who would look me square in the eyes and ask, "John, why are you choosing to do that? Have you spent time in prayer about that? What will moving accomplish that you cannot accomplish where you are? Is Anne 100% on board with this?"

We each need a truth-teller in our lives, but we also need a godly, "truth-asker." These are equally rare and they don't just happen. If you don't have a friend like this, you may need to take the initiative with one of your close friends with an invitation and permission: "I'd love to get your input occasionally on my money choices, and you will have my unconditional permission to ask me anything you want and tell me the truth." Don't be surprised if that friend not only agrees, but asks you to do the same for them." What a gift to have a friend like that.

#5 - GODLY COUNSEL

Every church has those who offer counsel. They're usually older. Possibly retired. They're faithful in attendance and often serve on various committees and boards. They may have an iPad, but they still carry their Bibles to church, and if you peeked inside its pages you'd see copious notes in the margins and multiple passages underlined. I know the Bible says all believers are saints, but these are the special saints of the church. I think you know who I'm talking about, and I'm pretty sure they would love to have you seek them out occasionally for godly counsel.

In 2011, as I was thinking through my recent transition from the financial advisory world to the non-profit world, I felt God leading me to seek some sage advice. I knew of a man in town who had a heart for God, a discerning ear, uncommon wisdom, and a history of prayer that could only be built over decades on his knees. It turns out I had been carrying his name and number in my wallet. You might have one of these names in your wallet or purse, too—the person you feel God wants you to call but you just haven't gotten around to it.

So I gave this man a call and went to see him. After some chit-chat he wanted to hear my story. He was in no hurry, so for an hour or so I talked and he listened carefully, asked a few clarifying questions, and jotted a few notes as I shared. I talked about where I had been professionally, where I was and where

I thought God was leading. Again, I was looking for input, not permission; guidance, not a decision.

Then he prayed. I mean really prayed. I'm not sure how long I sat there listening to him pray for me, for wisdom, for clarity, for my family, for my clients, for those in my future, for my strength and courage, and for the choices that lay in front of me. It was powerful. I didn't want to hear the "amen;" I wanted to sit there in the peace and hear his prayers. It was as if I were borrowing from his faith and his spiritual maturity—that somehow I got to share in his favor with God. I can't really explain it but I felt lighter when he finished, like my concerns were in the right perspective—God's perspective, not mine.

As we finished, we had three clear thoughts of how God may be leading me into this transition. All three were ministry focused and would be impactful. We both felt strongly about one of the options. (As it turned out, I ultimately took the boldest choice, which was not the one I was leaning toward when I left that day!) My time with this man created a faith-filled confidence in my choices, so much so that I knew I could not make a poor choice. Again, I was looking for input, wise counsel, and godly guidance, but the ultimate decision was between me and God.

Experience is a great teacher, and when combined with a heart for God you have an invaluable resource. Pay attention, because in the symmetry of God's economy, you may become someone else's godly counsel in the not-too-distant future.

#6 - YOUR PASTOR (OR CHRISTIAN LEADER)

The word pastor comes from a Latin word that means "shepherd." The role of a shepherd is to keep his sheep out of trouble by guiding them to safe places. It is not by accident that Jesus is often referred to as the Good Shepherd, or that the Book of Isaiah reports that, "All we like sheep have gone astray" (Isaiah 53:6, KJV). We all need an earthly shepherd to guide us to safe places, and your pastor serves that role. Whether it's the senior pastor or, if you attend a large church, one of the associate pastors, these godly shepherds offer yet another resource for your financial decision-making. Sometimes you may not have a traditional pastor, so look for a Christian leader who shepherds..

When I mention this resource to some people, they shrug, "We don't even know our pastor." That's a fair point, but I always press back: "What are you doing about that?" Pastors truly care about their flock, but they can't read your mind. And they also can't be everywhere at once. At least introduce yourself. Offer

> *Pastors truly care about their flock, but they can't read your mind.*

to meet him or her for lunch. Email the church office and make an appointment. Many of the larger churches in North America have stewardship pastors whose job it is to help people with their money matters and giving journeys.

Pastors bring at least three benefits to the table. First, they have a strong knowledge of the Bible—most are formally trained in biblical theology and doctrine. The best solutions to your money issues will always come from the Bible. Second, they have answered God's call to serve others in His name. Your pastor has your best interests in mind. He or she will tell you what's best for you, even if it's news you don't want to hear. Third, you can expect confidentiality. What's discussed in your pastor's office should stay there.

If you do not have a close relationship with your pastor or one of his associates, begin cultivating one today. It could be as simple as saying, "Pastor, from time to time I would love to be able to get your input on some of the decisions that are important to my spouse and me." I don't know a pastor who would turn down an opportunity to shepherd you through those decisions.

#7 - GOD'S CHURCH

When you made the decision to follow Christ, you joined His church. Not just a local church, but the very bride of Christ—a movement of followers around the world who are doing their best to serve Him and others. If nothing else, knowing that you're not alone—that there are others just like you struggling with the same things you do—can be a source of strength and encouragement.

Life is best lived out in the local church. I'm not suggesting you stand up in church and unload your money issues. But you can do more than just go to church on Sunday—you can *be* the church. Get involved in a small group. Build relationships. Volunteer in areas where your gifts and talents would be useful. Take advantage of special opportunities for learning.

> *Life is best lived out in the local church.*

Many churches offer adult education classes that provide guidance in everything from parenting to money management. As you immerse yourself in the life of the church, you will gain new friends, meet other families going through the same things you're experiencing, and find those godly men and women who can mentor you, and many will learn from you instead!

Relying on *The Seven* will not solve your money issues overnight. You may have been trying to take control for many years, and it will take a little while to get you where you want to be. But the next time you wake up in the middle of the night in a cold sweat over your finances you will begin to calm down as you realize you're not alone anymore. God is always awake and so you use this time to talk to Him.

> *Whatever worries wake you up at night are not bigger than the God who loves you.*

The person sleeping next to you is now your financial partner, too. You could wake him or her up and they could comfort you, reassure you that everything is going to work out. Or you could reach for your Bible and turn to God's promises to care for you, and provide for all of your needs. The couple sitting next to you in church may be going through the same thing. In fact, you've now become really close and have committed to sharing your journeys with each other. Your eyes begin falling shut as you rest in the knowledge that God has provided you with more than enough help to get to a better place.

Whatever worries wake you up at night are not bigger than the God who loves you. Like Annie sang, indeed, "the sun will come out tomorrow." Its light and warmth are God's reminders that you can trust him completely. And as you do, he will give you more than you can ever imagine.

REFLECTION

CHANGE FOR YOUR DOLLAR

1) No matter how foolish or desperate you feel about your financial situation, you can be assured others are facing the same struggles.
2) The Bible speaks to money issues so much because everyone faces its temptation for distraction.
3) No matter your situation, God has provided resources to help guide you. Using *The Seven* will guide you on the right track.
4) You were not intended to go it alone. Turn to God and those He puts in your path to help you seek His will.

MONEY IN MOTION

1) Write down your #1 priority in life.
2) Identify the characteristics you would want in someone who is in *The Seven* for you. Think about how you could

fulfill that role for someone else.

3) Develop a simple plan of reading, noting, and prayer. o
Make a plan for what you have to change to make God
a priority at the dawn of each day and think about how
that practice could help more than just your financial
choices during the day.

PRAYER

You chose the twelve to accompany you and learn from you. At the perfect time you sent them out in pairs to strengthen, challenge and pray for each other as they became your apostles. I've tried to do this on my own. I've let my pride get in the way of my transparency with my spouse and those who love me. I'm tired but I need the kind of rest that can only be found in you and received from those who love you. Help me recognize those you have placed around me to guide me in your way. Amen.

taking control

"He must become greater; I must become less."
The one who comes from above is above all;
the one who is from the earth belongs to the earth,
and speaks as one from the earth.
The one who comes from heaven is above all.
—John 3:30-31

If you've spent even a few Sundays in church, you've heard it: God has a plan for your life. It's one of those Christian nuggets we're fond of repeating—to others, to ourselves. We have been taught that God's plan will help us, not harm us (see Jeremiah 29:11), and that if we trust His plan and not our own, things will be a lot better for us (see Proverbs 3:5-6). We learn that God can do *more* for us than anything we could even think of or ask for (see Ephesians 3:20). In fact, apart from His plans for us, we can do nothing (see John 15:5). If I've heard it once, I've heard it a hundred times: God has a plan for me, and if I submit to it—if I trust and obey it—my life will be significantly better than if I stick to my own plan.

So, knowing that God's plan is best for me, why do I insist on *my* plan? Why do so many of us eventually reach a point (we always do) where we confess, "It's not working; I never thought it would be like this." Why is it that when we know God's still, small voice is more trustworthy than the enemy's whisper, we still listen to the whisper? Because the whisper often makes common sense. Notice, I didn't say the whisper was true, but the whisper always seems to line up with what the rest of the world is telling us. That shouldn't surprise you. The enemy is the prince of this world, so of course his messaging lines up. To win

> *The last thing I want is to get what I deserve.*

the battle for your attention, the enemy knows he doesn't have to kill you, that would be much to messy and draw much too much attention. No, all he needs to do is just distract you. That's right—just distract you. "Hey! Look over here, not at God!" Not a very high bar is it? So he whispers, "Why limit yourself when there's so much more you can have?" He tells us that God couldn't possibly mean it when He said you couldn't have that bright, shiny, delicious apple. Some have even turned this lie into a convincing theology: "Your heavenly father owns the cattle on a thousand hills. (see Psalm 50:10). He wants you to have a share in all that wealth. As a child of the King, you deserve it." You *deserve* it. That's a dangerous notion. As a follower of Christ, sinner, and money-mistaker extraordinaire, the last thing I want is to get what I deserve.

When we started out in our little Eden, we trusted God's plan even if we didn't know it. We had little to nothing, so it was easy to trust God because what we had was great: food, friends, and fun. Who could possibly ask for more? But then we looked around and saw others who had things we didn't have. Comparison destroyed our contentment, and that's when we made the choice. God's plan is fine for all that church stuff, but we better get going on a plan of our own for the other parts of our lives or we're gonna be left behind. We need to catch up. Everyone else is getting ahead of us. That was the moment. We stuck our shovels in the dirt and began building our little "k" kingdoms.

HEY! LOOK OVER HERE!

It's not that we blatantly disobeyed God or rebelled against Him. We still wanted to follow His plan but thought we needed our own little backup plan for insurance. God's plan promised most of what we wanted: peace, joy, fulfillment, and best of all, eternal life. But it didn't seem to include *all* of what we wanted, so naturally we felt it was up to us to figure out how we were going to afford that bigger house, the second car, and the closets full of stuff that good, hard-working people like us deserved. There's that "d" word again.

Our plan may have been built partially on a lie—a lie that told us God was holding out on us, that there was more to be experienced, and that happiness and satisfaction could be found in many places other than God, and could especially come from what we owned. The world's plan is built on a lie; God's plan is built on His truth. The truth that everything we need comes from Him. And everything means *everything*. Because the world's plans are built on a lie, they never work. It might look like it is working for a while, that's the enemy at his best, giving you the feeling of success and pride in your choices. Yet, before too long, trying to live by both our plan and God's plan always ends badly because they are not parallel. Our plan is on a different trajectory and progressively takes us farther and farther away from God's plan.

> *The world's plan is built on a lie; God's plan is built on His truth.*

Our plan also gives us results we desire, and initially they seems to be not only harmless but enormously attractive. Our plan gives us what we want. What could be cooler than that? You want the car? Sign and drive. You want the new living room furniture? Six years same as cash. You want the time share? It will actually make you money! None of these things in and of themselves are bad, but they have a tendency to create a divide between you and God. At first, the obstacles aren't that big. With a little effort, you can get around them. But as you keep following your plan, they get bigger, wider, thicker, and then finding your way back to God's plan gets more difficult. In your heart, you know you need His plan, and you try hard to get back to it, but now you're getting tired. The results of your plan require a lot of work; all that stuff needs your attention. And even if it doesn't demand your attention, its hooks are set in your world and will slow you down and trip you up. You still want God's plan, but following your own plan has depleted all your energy. Eventually, the obstacles that result from your plan surround you

> *Money is the universal barrier to God.*

until you are separated from God's plans, when you thought yours could go alongside His. You have just illustrated the sobering thought expressed by bestselling author, John Piper: "Money is the universal barrier to God." You are now a full-fledged, loyal serf in your little "k" kingdom." You have traded everything you love for what you thought you wanted. You got some cool stuff, but what did you lose in the process?

If you look at the graph on the next page, you will see an over-simplified illustration of this trajectory of God's plan versus our plans. Not only are the plans moving in different directions, God's plan is always superior to our own. Unfortunately, as we move farther along in our plan, traps set by the enemy begin to separate us from God's plans. Hazards of life occur that can separate us as well if we do not keep them in the proper context. But I find the most costly separators from God's plans are our very own choices and actions and the barriers they create. And when we finally realize these facts, we will also find that navigating ourselves back to God's plan can feel difficult. We will have to navigate around the traps, avoid the hazards, and ultimately we will need to tear down the barriers we built. It may seem imposing, but God is there and He is calling us to Him every moment of every day and He can make your path straight in the speed of prayer.

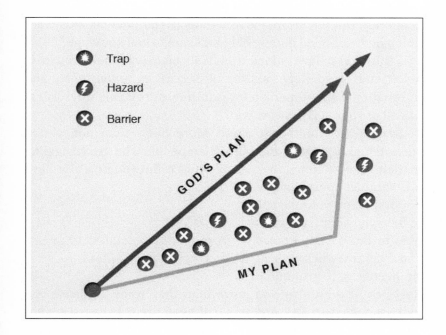

Following God's plan always produces what is best for us. Always. The Bible often uses the word *blessings* to describe the benefits of following God's plan. Not exactly a twenty-first century term, but it literally means to offer something really good to someone. That's what we can count on when we follow God's plan: something better for us than we could provide for ourselves.

And God is able to bless you abundantly, so that in all things at all times, having all that you need, you will abound in every good work.
—2 Corinthians 9:8

In his book, *Treat Me Like a Customer*, author Lewis Upkins shared a conversation he had with an acquaintance who had built a hugely successful business. As he poured himself into his business, he provided his family with all the best that money could buy. But when Upkins asked his friend how his kids were doing he responded glumly, "My kids don't even know me."

With all you have gained from your plan, what have you lost? My friend Lloyd Reeb, author of *Success to Significance*, and international spokesperson for Halftime, puts it this way: "What has all of your success cost you?"

Remember, you're not alone. More likely than not, you're surrounded by a lot of good Christian people who are struggling in their little "k" kingdoms just as you are. But you now also have a reliable support team— *The Seven*—in your corner to help you shift from your plan to God's plan. Prayer and scripture will keep you connected and grounded.

> *Could it be that God asks us to live our life in modesty so that we are prepared to give our life in extravagance?*

Real people who love God more than they want to please you will keep you focused. And you will need them, because it's not going to be easy. The enemy will continue to whisper and look for opportune moments to tempt you with your own plan, and his message will be, "Look over here at all the flashy, beautiful things. Not over there at God and His plan." His allies in a culture obsessed with more will continue to make you feel incomplete if you do not have (fill in the blank).

Your plan says more is more. God's plan says less is more. Less you, more Him. Could it be that God asks us to live our life in modesty so we are prepared to give our life in extravagance?

LESS WORLD, MORE GOD

On the surface, God's plan doesn't make sense. That's because it's counter intuitive. If I want more of something, well, I need to get more. Not less. If I want more financial freedom, I need to get more money, right? If I want my kids to have a better life than I had, I need to get them what I never had. Says who?

It doesn't help that this message is reinforced by a culture obsessed with bigger, better and more of it along with delivery systems that keep that message in front of us 24-7. The highly-respected Yankelovich market research firm reports that the average person sees approximately 5,000 advertising messages a day.[5] Everywhere you turn, something is shouting: "You can't live without this!" When you grab one of those bins to put your stuff in before you go through airport security, you see an ad staring up at you. Believe it or not, that advertiser gets your attention this way.

According to the firm Supply Marketing, Disney advertised its Little Einsteins DVDs for preschoolers on the paper liners of exam rooms in 2,000 pediatricians' offices. Not to be indelicate, but you can't even go to the bathroom without seeing the benefits of more—a company called Wizmark (you can't make this stuff up) places ads above those porcelain things that men stand in front of in public restrooms.

But don't blame advertisers. They're just giving us what we want: information on how to get more. They wouldn't do it if it didn't work. Advertising works because we can't get that whisper out of our minds.

To shift from our plan to God's we have to believe His truth that less is more—less world, more God. To quote James Earl Jones playing the character of Terrence Mann in the movie *Field of Dreams*, he summed it up in a few powerful words referring to the American public, "for it's money they have, it's peace they lack."

> *Advertising works because we can't get that whisper out of our minds.*

It sounds good on paper, but how does it work in real life? How do you break free from the money myth that says if you just had a little more you'd be happy? It's not easy because your money problems are not about your money. You and your spouse can decide to spend less money and still miss the freedom and joy that comes from living by God's plan rather than yours. That's because your money problems are not a financial issue, but a spiritual one. Your finances usually don't change much until you do, and the apostle Paul seems to echo that when he wrote, "*do not conform any longer to the pattern of this world, but be transformed by the renewing of your mind*" (Romans 12:1).

Long before we begin to act differently, we need to think differently. Every financial decision I made that I thought would make my life better conformed to "the pattern of this world." I did what everyone around me—Christian or not—was doing. It made perfect sense, even though it did not deliver what I thought it would.

The new way of thinking that Paul urges us to consider gives us the ability to evaluate our financial decisions against God's plan rather than ours:

> *Then you will be able to test and approve what God's will is—his good, pleasing, and perfect will.*
> —Romans 12:2

Imagine the impact this will have on how you both spend money. Instead of buying the leather couch as everyone else buys a leather couch, you now have a new perspective. Your friends will shop around for the best price. They will look for a couch that fits the decor of their home. They might go online to read customer reviews. And then they'll make their decision. You may perform the same due diligence, but you now have an added criterion, one that comes from God's plan instead of your own: Do we want to upgrade our furniture because all of our friends recently upgraded their living rooms? Or do we want this because we really need it? We want our most heartfelt desires to please God and to honor Him with our resources.

Long before we begin to act differently, we need to think differently.

But John, are you really saying that God cares about my

couch? Not specifically, though the Bible tells us He numbers the hair on our heads. (see Luke 12:7) I take that to mean He knows us intimately and cares about the little things as well as the big things. What He *does* care about is your heart. He wants a relationship with you more than He wants you to own a leather couch. And if He senses that the couch will get in the way of that relationship, His Holy Spirit will caution you through an inner voice (see John 16:13), your conscience (see Romans 9:1), or through other means. You may really, really want it, but something inside just won't feel right. So in that context, God does care about your couch, or your car, or your house, or anything else that has the potential to come between you and Him.

> *We want our most heartfelt desires to please God and to honor Him with our resources.*

For you to hear and obey the Holy Spirit, something has to change, and that something is you. If you're hiking in the woods and you recognize you're on the wrong path, what do you do? You change paths. One reason money may have become such a problem for you and your spouse is that you may have been running on the wrong path. Instead of asking, "How can we find more money to support our lifestyle?," you both may need to ask a more telling question, such as: "How much is enough?"

HOW MUCH IS ENOUGH?

If your answer is a number, then you didn't fully understand the question. And you likely will never have enough. From a financial perspective, all it takes is a few clicks of inflation, a drop in the value of your investments, a CEO's decision to downsize. You can't guard the economy, but you can guard your heart. To Jesus, the widow's mite was enough because it represented a total commitment. The rich people may have given quantitatively more, but proportionately, it was only a small portion of their wealth. Their plan said I have to be careful. God doesn't want me to run out of money. It costs a lot to run my kingdom. The widow trusted God's plan that says you can't serve two masters (see Matthew 6:24). It's either all in or not at all, but if you go all in with me I will give you the desires of your heart (See Proverbs 3:5-6).

> *You can't guard the economy, but you can guard your heart.*

How much money or stuff does it take to interrupt a person's relationship with God?

- For Eve, all it took was an apple.
- For Judas, it was thirty pieces of silver.
- For the foolish farmer, it was a barn full of grain.
- For the rich young ruler, it was all the wealth he had amassed.
- *What about you?*

We do need to be careful with the question, "How much is enough?" I believe it's a good question, but maybe not a complete question. Conceptually, it's simple to understand, but I believe it can often leave too much open for interpretation. "How much is enough" . . . *for what?*

- How much is enough . . . so we will never run out of money?
- How much is enough . . . so we can do everything we want to do?
- How much is enough . . . so we can remain steadfast in God's will?
- The list goes on and on . . .

There are lots of ways to end that question, so if you use it, make sure you are clear on how you qualify it. I think a another way to phrase the "How much is enough?" question would encompass something like this, "How do we steward what we have to honor God and love our neighbor, living well within His provision for us, while remaining open to his calling on our lives?" God gives us a very simple answer in Hebrews 13:5: *Keep your lives free from the love of money and be content with what you have, because God has said, "Never will I leave you; never will I forsake you."* Regardless how you ask yourself this question, you *do* need to ask yourself this question, but approach it from God's perspective and His answer will be revealed.

ALL WE NEED

When Jesus was teaching a huge crowd of people and he noticed they were hungry, the disciples went into their little "k" kingdom mode and came up with a solution that made sense: We better send them home so they can get something to eat." But Jesus had other ideas and said, "They don't need to go home. Just give them something to eat." Still following their own plan, they reminded Jesus that they didn't have enough food—only a few loaves of bread and some fish. According to their plan, it

> *"Enough" is not about cutting back or living within a budget. It's about recognizing that God is provision.*

wasn't enough, but under God's plan, it was more than enough. What they had was enough. Less became more.

God's plan has a way of turning things upside down. In our way of thinking, success is having what you want. In God's economy, success is wanting what you have. Enough is not about cutting back or living within a budget. It's about recognizing that God is provision. Everything we need comes from Him (see James 1:17). Or to put it another way, He is *all* we need: "*The Lord is my shepherd, I shall not be in want*" (Psalm 23:1). In our little Eden, we had all that we needed. It was enough. When we begin looking at how much is enough rather than how to afford more, we will reclaim the joy and freedom that characterize those early more simple years.

Long before I met with my mentor and friend, and soon after I made my decision to leave my financial practice and launch the Piedmont office of the National Christian Foundation, I made an even tougher decision—to tell Anne that I thought we needed to downsize from our dream home to something smaller, in case God did lead us to make this job move, so the expense and upkeep of our house would not be a barrier. That was going to be a tough conversation. I was asking my wife to move . . . again.

A lot went through my mind before I had that conversation. I prayed for awhile to get the courage and the words. Anne didn't sign up for this conversation, yet she was getting it. She married a guy who wanted to be successful and wanted to give her all the trappings that came along with that. It's not that she ever asked for them; I just wanted to give them to her, and my drive for money and success matched my plans to please her. I had grown up in Christian home, but in the early days of our marriage, I was not necessarily pursuing Christ.

> *The money may decrease so the mission must increase.*

You see, when I met Anne, my hunt for my bride was over. Stick a fork in me, I was done! Here was a beautiful girl who was way above my pay grade and seemed to not mind looking at me . . . and she laughed at my jokes. It was time for this country boy to stop looking.

That was over thirty years ago and she has put up with a lot of financial nonsense with me—successes and failures, financial health and financial sickness. You get the point. And here I was getting ready to ask her to move again. As Ruth Graham once said when asked if she ever thought of divorcing her husband, Billy, she replied, "Divorce? No. Murder? Yes!" Lord, help me.

As God would have it, the conversation went as well as it could go and was not without some tears from both of us. We eventually came to a really good place and began to make plans for getting our house on the market. It was 2011 and not a good market in our town, but our house sold for a good price. Not what we were asking, but a good price. We estimate that we took about a 20% haircut on the sale price and left a significant amount of money on the table. Following God on your financial journey gets interesting. Your numbers may not always add up on the balance sheet, but they always add up in God's economy. The money may decrease so the mission may increase.

In the movie, *Facing the Giants*, there is a memorable exchange in the school hallway, outside the coach's office, between Coach Grant Taylor (Alex Kendrick) and Mr. Bridges (Ray Wood). It had great impact on me and it goes like this:

> Mr. Bridges: *"Grant, I heard a story about two farmers who desperately needed rain, and both of them prayed for rain, but only one of them went out and prepared his fields to receive it. Which one do you think trusted God to send the rain?"*
>
> Coach Taylor: *"Well, the one who prepared his fields for it."*
>
> Mr. Bridges: *"Which one are you?"*
>
> Coach Taylor: *(stands speechless in thought)*

I love the faithful courage the farmer displayed in this story as he prepared his fields while he prayed for rain, while the other farmer was fearful and kept his seeds dry in the barn. When the rain finally came, only the seeds that had been planted began to grow, and I have to believe his harvest was magnificent!

Before we closed on our house sale we found a smaller house with a smaller yard and smaller expenses and smaller upkeep. We "prepared our fields." We wound up moving in about five months before God confirmed our choice to leave my practice and launch the ministry. The barrier of the house was gone, the path was clear, and we felt in the center of His will.

As I built my business based on sales goals and with it my little "k" kingdom, I made many financial decisions based on what others would think of me. I wanted to look successful and gain the approval of others. According to my own plan, the way to do that was to accumulate more. It never occurred to me that having less would be a benefit then, and in the future. Less to distract, less to pay for, less to impress. God's plan offers the only true way to gain the respect and admiration of others. *"For the kingdom of God is not a matter of eating or drinking [lifestyle], but of righteousness, peace and joy in the Holy Spirit, because anyone who serves Christ in this way is pleasing to God and approved by men"* (Romans 14:17-18).

> God's plan offers the only true way to gain the respect and admiration of others.

If you really want others to look up to you, place your trust in God and live according to His plan. Remember my friend who has the lovely property that he shares so generously with others? He's extremely wealthy. I appreciate the fact that he has worked hard to build such a successful and rewarding business, but I respect him more for his obedience to Christ and his love for others. When you are completely sold out to Jesus, people will be drawn to you and the peace and joy that they see in you, not what you own.

If in God's plan less is more, and if you desire to abandon your plan for His, what does that mean in practical terms? Do you need to follow our Lord's advice to the rich young ruler and get rid of everything? Shane Claiborne is a young author who writes and speaks a lot about the hold our stuff has on our hearts and souls. Once he was speaking to a group shortly after the house he lived in burned. As he shared that bit of news with his audience, (and that everyone was safe from the fire), he said with a sly grin, as only someone who has been through that kind of tragedy can do, "I think it would be a good thing for all of us if that happened every three or four years." Shane wasn't really saying house fires are a good thing, and Jesus wasn't telling everyone to sell all we have and give to the poor. But, he used this story to warn us about making our money and wealth more important than Him, more important than salvation. We all have these "rich young ruler" questions in our lives. These questions are directed toward our idols that are beginning to become more important than Jesus. Choose wisely.

As I was getting close to the end of my career as an advisor, I was in Atlanta visiting the ministry I was likely going to be joining within the next twelve months. My practice was still in full swing and I was actively serving my clients. During a break between some meetings I decided to check my email. As I read a short email from a very special couple, a flood of memories came roaring back of my journey with them.

I met Bob and Jane (not their real names) about a dozen years earlier. They were both launching their careers, one as a doctor and one as an attorney. They were young and fresh, starting life together and living free. They didn't have very much, and even if they did they would not have had the time to enjoy it. Young professionals are not known for keeping forty-hour workweeks. They were overworked, underpaid, but they had joy between the two of them. The only way they could make ends meet was for Bob to work additional hours to earn some extra cash.

I loved working with them. They were smart, they were coachable, and they wanted to start out on the right foot with their finances. I covered all the basics with them and they were off and running. They were good at it to. It wasn't long before they were in a healthy rhythm of annual review and planning. They did two things very well, 1) They kept a summary—all they owned, debts, income, expenses, savings, taxes, insurance, and a few other details—that was updated each year, and 2) they always gave me a call to brainstorm about any major financial revisions or decisions. So I was not surprised to get a call from

Bob one winter day.

They had just gotten back from a snow skiing vacation with some friends and they had seen a house for sale. It was right on the slopes. Ski in; ski out. Paradise. It was expensive, but if they all went in on the house together, they could easily afford it by using their budgeted vacation fund to pay for it. It's all they talked about with their friends the whole vacation. They could go on the weekends, pick weeks to go together, and best of all, the realtor told them they could rent this perfect house for enough money to cover almost all of the mortgage and property taxes. Shopping for real estate on vacation is like shopping for groceries when you're hungry—you might buy something you don't need.

> *Shopping for real estate on vacation is like shopping for groceries when you're hungry—you might buy something you don't need.*

Bob had already run it by his CPA who was all for this new investment, but it had been Bob's habit to call me to talk about things like this as well. I quietly listened as he pitched me on the idea. The math worked, as it usually does in these examples. This is a good time to remember what we talked about earlier in the book: There is a place where math stops and you begin. It was a good deal with a great upside. I echoed everything the CPA had shared. Then I walked through some additional very reasonable financial questions I wanted them to consider. You may have even asked yourself questions like this in the past. Interestingly, this solid financial guidance has its roots in biblical wisdom.

"Bob, what would happen if . . ."
- . . . you cosigned the loan and the other couple ran into financial difficulty, or worse, got divorced?
  - o *Root* - God tells us Proverbs 22:26 not to "shake hands in pledge for debts" unless we are prepared to pay for the whole thing.
- . . . the resort went through a light snow season and the

rentals were not as good as you planned?

- o *Root* - God warns us to not to presume upon the future in James 4:13.
- • . . . you couldn't sell the house if you needed to and you got stuck with it and the payments?
  - o *Root* - God tells us in Proverbs 22:7 that "the borrower becomes the servant of the lender."
- • . . . as the kids got older, they didn't want to hang out with mom and dad at the house on the slopes any more, and your vacation needs changed?
  - o *Root* - God tells us in Ephesians 6:4 "not to exasperate our children but train them gently . . ."

Like all great financial wisdom, the most common financial truths we use every day have their root firmly planted in the soil of God's word.

Bob made his decision and was not looking forward to telling Jane. I might not have been a popular person with them at that moment. But time passed, they did not buy the house, and they put their extra money into their current mortgage to accelerate its payoff. That was number of years ago. Honestly, I had forgotten about it until I got the following email. It was short and sweet and read something like this:

Dear John,

I just wanted to say thank you for your help over the years. I wanted to let you know that we sent in our last mortgage payment today. We are now 100% debt free.

Thanks!
Bob

They were in their early forties when they sent that email. No debt. No lenders in control of their financial lives. They could vacation anywhere they wanted, including the ski slopes! And, as a bonus, they dodged the unanticipated impact of the largest economic disaster in recent history. For Bob and Jane, less was truly more.

For the rest of us, less is more may mean simply having an honest conversation with our spouses about all the stuff we have and all the stuff we think we want. It could also include a straightforward look at the amount of time and energy that goes into sustaining or increasing your current standard of living.

So often I see couples who chose their lifestyle before they chose their life. I often meet couples who bought their houses before they thought about their homes. And many chose the pursuit of wealth by mostly abandoning the pursuit of Christ. As my dad says, this is the point where I go "from preachin' to meddlin'!" Here are a few conversation starters I've used in the past (worksheet online on FREE page):

- To what end are you working so hard?
- In your efforts to gain, what are you losing?
- How much of your efforts are going solely to yourself? How much to serving others?
- What message are you giving your children if you give them more things but less time?
- What is your lifestyle communicating to your children about money?
- How would you rate your joy when you had less, compared to now when you have so much more?
- What do you own that you don't really need, and what is it costing us to keep it?
- What would it take to decrease your spending budget by ten percent? Twenty percent?
- What percentage of your spending is based on what you have to pay, need to pay, or want to pay?
- If you could sell your house for a profit and purchase a smaller one, would you do it? Why, or why not?

- To what extent are your financial decisions influenced by what others think? By what God thinks?
- What role does generosity and giving play in your new plans?

These are simple but serious questions, and all are money moments—real life situations involving our money with underlying motives and messages guiding our choices, resulting in real consequences.

When we love God and His plans for us more than we love our own plans, one of the most beautiful consequences of a "less is more" attitude is the effect is has on our generosity and giving. Sometimes this can be very natural, but it always needs to be intentional.

> *But since you excel in everything—in faith, in speech, in knowledge, in complete earnestness and in the love we have kindled in you—see that you also excel in this grace of giving.*
> —2 Corinthians 8:7

We are to be obedient to the word of God in our generosity, as sacrificial as the life of Christ, and as powerful as the Holy Spirit that guides our lives, with our giving aimed at heaven to "*take hold of the life that is truly life*" (see 1 Timothy 6:17-19). Our giving is reflected in many areas of our lives, but it is especially evident as we worship and love God with our financial gifts to His Church. Our financial fruitfulness is one tangible way to show love to our neighbor, taking care of those in need, and bringing glory to God. Could it be that easy to point our hearts toward God and His plans for us? Luke says it is.

> *For where your treasure is, there your heart will be also.*
> —Luke 12:34

As I counsel families, this wisdom of generosity, combined

with all of the wisdom of God, often flies directly in the face of conventional wisdom. His wisdom tells us that our financial choices must align with

> The fact that God's wisdom does not make worldly sense is not my problem, it's my salvation.

our faith and our faith must align with what He commands. This counsel usually creates two types of problems: my problems and not my problems. The fact that God's wisdom does not make worldly sense is not my problem, it's my salvation.

As often is the fact, God cuts to the heart of the matter as only He can do:

> *For the message of the cross is foolishness to those who are perishing, but to us who are being saved it is the power of God. For it is written: "I will destroy the wisdom of the wise; the intelligence of the intelligent I will frustrate." Where is the wise person? Where is the teacher of the law? Where is the philosopher of this age? Has not God made foolish the wisdom of the world? For since in the wisdom of God the world through its wisdom did not know Him, God was pleased through the foolishness of what was preached to save those who believe. Jews demand signs and Greeks look for wisdom, but we preach Christ crucified: a stumbling block to Jews and foolishness to Gentiles, but to those whom God has called, both Jews and Greeks, Christ the power of God and the wisdom of God. For the foolishness of God is wiser than human wisdom, and the weakness of God is stronger than human strength.*
>
> —1 Corinthians 1:18-25 NIV

REFLECTION

CHANGE FOR YOUR DOLLAR

1) It is too easy to find external justification for internal desires when we ignore God's voice.
2) Our instinct is to gather, to collect, to amass, and to preserve. God wants us to sow, to reap, to give away, to release. We think our path will lead to more, but God's path is the only way to true abundance.
3) You will never have enough as long as you are allowing the world to be the gauge by which you measure.
4) Don't choose your lifestyle before you choose your life. It will make it much more difficult to navigate from your plan to God's.

MONEY IN MOTION

1) If you own an item that is a distraction think about when you acquired it, if you are planning to keep it, and what your motivation is for that decision.
2) Think about the things in your life that have become a barrier to God and whether you have the courage to tear them down.
3) Look for ways to create less world and more God in your life. Find someone in your life who can hold you accountable for this choice.
4) Try to identify what you have in your life that may be blocking your view of God.
5) Determine whether you are giving at the level you feel you should. If not, look at ways you can gradually increase your giving.

PRAYER

Lord, forgive me. I have accumulated so much in comparison to the rest of the world. Yet, I look around me and there are others who have so much more. My sight is so limited and your Kingdom is so massive. Let me be the blessing that you desire me to be. Help me to know you will always be all I will ever need. Amen.

IX

recapturing life

And He died for all, that those who live should no longer live for themselves but for Him who died for them and was raised again.
—2 Corinthians 5:15

I was in China a few years ago and was looking for directions on a building map. I knew where I was headed, but I needed to know where I was in the building. I found the ever-familiar red dot on the map and beside was not the familiar "You are here." Instead, it read, "You are in the position of now." With a smile and a chuckle I was off to my meeting. The translation wasn't perfect, but it was so true.

When you are headed to a destination, you have to know two things—*where you are and where you want to go.* If you only know where you are, it's good information, but it only defines here. On the other hand, if you only know where you want to go, you can easily lose sight of your current situation in relation to *there.*

> *When you are headed to a destination, you have to know two things—where you are and where you want to go.*

Therefore, if you only know one or the other, it can be difficult, if not impossible, to plan. As we walk through this chapter, I want to focus on where you are and the foundation to be built before we seek to start a new journey. We will concentrate on the *financial* choices that may be affecting your *life* choices.

But we must be mindful at every step.

If we don't have the right plan in place—God's plan—it really doesn't matter how skillfully we are able to use the resources that God has provided. Why would we want to use our resources on the wrong plan? We want to use the right plan and the right resources applied to them to bring God glory. In *My Utmost for His Highest*, Oswald Chamber shares that "when our natural power of sight is devoted and submitted in obedience to the Holy Spirit, it will become the very power by which we perceive God's will, and our entire life is kept in simplicity."

> God's plan + God's resources + our obedience =
> unfathomable eternal impact

God wants us here, focused on today, yet open to Him and where He wants to take us. Your questions will ultimately be: Will I be prepared and able to go when He calls? As a *mist that appears for a little while and then vanishes*, (see James 4:1-13), we have only a short time to accomplish what God has planned. Your wealth can be a blessing or a barrier to God and His plans.

To help with this ever-present tension, we want to begin to build a guide, a source of thoughtful information that can point you in the right direction today and into the future—a guide to *strengthen* your convictions, *prompt* reflection of beliefs, *identify* key values around your finances, and your intentions for your financial future. It will bring you closer to Christ and help you flourish without the influences of your finances dragging you down. To learn to use money as a tool that can glorify God and not a goal that may take you away from Him. It can provide a framework that reminds you that you are to steward all He has

> *God wants us here, focused on today, yet open to Him and where He wants to take us.*

given you to impact the culture for Him. You will also be able to identify any danger zones and past traps, so that when you approach those choices, you can know to be doubly on your guard, treading prayerfully and

> *The choice to follow God more closely is available to each of us every moment of every day.*

strategically in that space. You will want to capture every space and every opportunity for Christ! You ultimately will develop a Kingdom vision and a plan for the future, to guide your faith in action today and provide the framework for your financial choices—all in alignment with God's word and His plans for you.

But as with any journey, we can all get a little lost at one time or another. (As a guy, I will deny I ever said that. Anne says I am not necessarily lost; I just sometimes take the scenic route while not enjoying it!) Even with that marvelous piece of technology known as the GPS, we can still get off course. You could be driving down some unfamiliar road and realize you're heading in the wrong direction. You must have missed your turn. According to the GPS on your smartphone, you're on track, but you have your doubts. Something doesn't feel right. You don't seem to be getting closer to your destination. Emotions build with every recalculating announcement. Wasn't there supposed to be a Panera Bread on the left? Maybe you went right when you were supposed to stay straight at that last intersection. If you were lost before, now you really feel disoriented, and all you have to help you is a microchip-brained co-pilot. The question is so obvious. *Can you trust it?*

If you've hung with me this far, you may be thinking about making your own U-turn, deciding to redirect your path to follow God's plan instead of your own. In the Bible, in Greek, this *U-turn back to God, this changing of your mind* is best known as *metanoia*. I love knowing the choice to follow God more closely is available to each of us every moment of every day. So let's say you decide to make some changes. What now? Your plan may not have delivered what you thought it would, so you're pretty sure you're going to need to ditch it. That's a good call, but it won't be easy. More good news is that you still have your trustworthy resources—*The Seven.* You realize that the whisper you've been listening to gave you deadly advice. You may still hear the whisper, but now your desire is to listen to the still, small voice of God. The same questions come up again ... *but can you trust him?*

God is never wrong. You can completely trust His plans for you and of how you handle money. But don't be surprised if at times you wonder if you're on the right course. The enemy's tactics will become more precise and persistent because he doesn't want to lose you. The whispers get louder. The traps look more inviting. The barriers can get taller. And the hazards may come quicker. But God wins. Don't confuse the battles with the war (see John 16:33). Think progress, not perfection. You will have your moments of doubt. Some of your friends might think you're crazy. The allure of more will eventually begin to fade as you put your trust in Him. I've seen it happen in my own life and the lives of others.

IT'S TIME TO FIND YOUR NOW

It's time for focused action. You likely have a general idea of how things are, but that's not going to be enough any more. To make the necessary changes and reclaim the life you were meant to enjoy, you need to get specific. You get to take inventory and define reality. Then, gather the results of your inventory on paper and agree, just like the building map in China, "this is *our* red dot, this is our position of *now.*" After you define where you are today, then you can begin to plan your next steps, but remember who gets to direct them? Adventure awaits!

The mind of man plans his way, but the Lord directs his steps.
—Proverbs 16:9 NASB

FIND YOUR NOW (NOW) includes three thoughtful steps:

1) Define your near future over the next twelve months with The Stewardship Question (SQ),
2) Uncover the areas to celebrate, correct, add, and clarify with The Four Helpful Lists (4HL),
3) Identify, explore and expand the next best steps in your journey using "The ReNew Filter (RF).

(Before you begin, please print the CHAPTER IX GUIDE FORMS on the FREE page at JohnHPutnam.com.)

As my friend Lloyd Reeb often says, "It's time to get clear, get free and get going!" Ready to have some fun? I've been doing this a long time, and I have found that there are similar items that couples commonly need to define their NOW: clarity, unity, and context.

- Clarity—to define your current reality.
- Unity— to agree on that reality.
- Context—to identify and prioritize actions and next steps.

As you walk through these steps, take your time; there is no need to be in a hurry. Let the process work, and let God speak as you work. These next steps will help you create useful lists and records, which will also bring insights into your *money in motion* I introduced in Chapter I and the *Stewardship Specs* I introduced in Chapter III. We know that God is the master, not us. We are the stewards. As we get into less and get rid of more, we'll be getting clarity on His instructions, the resources

It's time to get clear, get free and get going!

we have, and the choices we've made. We need to record these answers because clarity protects us from the lies of the enemy— the villain of our stewardship journey. These lists help us see the enemy for who he is—a deceiver who wants to keep us trapped in our little "k" kingdoms. It also provides a framework so we can make clearer choices.

Creating our list is the easy part. We do it all the time, don't we? We make lists of things to do at work and at home. We write down our goals and objectives. And of course, there are those pesky New Year's resolutions. The deceptive thing about

> *Clarity protects us from the lies of the enemy.*

making lists is that it feels like we've done something. In reality, we haven't done anything except write some things on a piece of paper. The challenge is to turn these items into action.

FIND YOUR NOW
STEP #1: THE STEWARDSHIP QUESTION

For FIND YOUR NOW Step #1, I've borrowed from a concept from an organization called Strategic Coach. They call it the "The R Factor." It's basically a simple question, yet one of the most powerful ones I've ever used, and it leads to effective change: *"If we were meeting three years from today and you were to look back over those three years, what has to have happened during that period for you to feel happy about your progress?"* [6]

As I've used this question, I've shortened the time frame, changed the language, and I call this tool the Financial Stewardship Question (Financial SQ): *If we were sitting here a year from now—and you were to look back over the past twelve months—what had to have happened for you to feel confident in your stewardship of the financial resources that God has provided you?"* [6]

Pass #1 with the Financial SQ is going to be very natural and open-ended. As you ponder the question, write down any topics, ideas, or to-dos that come to mind. There are no wrong answers. As I tell people who are in the middle of this exercise, this is purely a "financial brain dump"—just write down whatever comes to mind. You might even come up with some items that are not specifically money related, that's okay. God may have put that on your mind for a specific reason, so write everything down.

Also, now is not the time to get too deep into the weeds and details of the items you are recording. Remember, we're just making the list now, don't try to fix anything. You will sense when the answers to this question slow down, and that is usually a natural ending to this step. As the answers begin to slow, now we will move to Pass #2 of the *Financial SQ* take specific areas of your *money in motion* and unpack each one of these in the same manner. This may feel a little redundant, but it will help ensure you've covered all of your financial bases. (As a reminder, the *money in motion* categories are: spend, save, invest, give, taxes, plan, and counsel.) As an example: Pass #2 of the *Financial SQ* with the *money in motion* categories will sound something like this: "*If we were sitting here a year from now—and you were to look back over the past twelve months—what had to have happened with your SPENDING to feel confident in your stewardship of what God has provided you?*" Some common replies to the *Financial SQ* may be:

- *Be more generous in our giving.*
- *Plan a date night every week or two.*
- *Stick to our budget.*
- *Have a budget!*
- *Save to go on a mission trip as a family.*
- *Hire a financial advisor.*

If you made it to this point, you have finished the *Financial SQ* in reviewing your finances and your *money in motion*. Congratulations! You are well on your way to laying the groundwork to recapture your life from your lifestyle. Before you move on to the next step, take a moment to read through the excellent work you've done up to this point. Now is a good time for a short break and share a thankful prayer!

FIND YOUR NOW
STEP #2: FOUR HELPFUL LISTS (4HL)

Next, for FIND YOUR NOW Step #2, we'll use my next favorite resource that I've adopted from the book, *Living the Life You Were Meant to Live*, by Tom Paterson. It's called the "Four Helpful Lists," (4HL) and it's a wonderful tool that I've used successfully hundreds of times. The four lists are:

- What's right?
- What's wrong?
- What's missing?
- What's confusing?

I know these questions may seem overly simple on the surface, but please bear with me. If you will take your time and give each question your prayerful, honest response, these four simple questions will lead to very powerful insights. In the *Financial 4HL*, we once again will to focus on our finances and money. As we practiced in the *Financial SQ* above, after you take Pass #1 through these questions, then go back through these lists with Pass #2 using the *money in motion* categories (spend, save, invest, give, taxes, plan, counsel) and ask each question again. There may be some repetition, but we want to put each category under the magnifying glass and take a good, long look. Have fun!

What's right with your finances and money? Any time you take inventory of any area of your life, you have the tendency to look at the gaps, the mistakes, and the things that need to be fixed. This is where the enemy wants you. The enemy wants you drowning in a glass half empty, discouraged and convinced that you're never going to get any better and can't get your life back. So begin your inventory by listing everything that's good and right in your financial life. These are the things that need to be celebrated! These are the things on your personal praise report.

After you make a list of all the things you've done right with your *money in motion*, and all the those things that are joyful, then celebrate that list. Be thankful and give yourself a high-five!

What's wrong in your finances and money? As you begin to make this list, think in terms of financial things in your life that need to be fixed or corrected. These are not necessarily bad by definition, but definitely need attention. Here's where you have to be really honest with yourself and give permission to your spouse to be honest with you. Keep in mind that a lot of the things that are "wrong" may have seemed like good choices. For example, You took the promotion and the raise because it was offered to you, but within a few weeks you realized the additional work and new responsibilities took you away from what you really loved about your job. Now you're in a job you really don't like, but you've already upgraded your lifestyle to fit your budget. In Lysa TerKeurst's bestselling book, *The Best Yes, How to Make Wise Decisions in the Midst of Endless Demands*, she focuses on our unique opportunity to choose the best over the good. The good demands in your life,

> The enemy wants you drowning in a glass half empty.

left unobserved, can begin to take up more and more of who you are and what you do, ultimately building a barrier between you and God. Lysa shares that we all want to save the "best yes" for God. Pay particular attention to the financial choices in your life where God doesn't seem present or that don't match up to His will. My friend Ron Blue's truth-telling bears repeating, "there are no financial problems, only spiritual ones."

Let me add a reminder here. As with the *Financial SQ*, when you record your responses, don't try to solve anything, don't analyze, don't prioritize or sort. And don't think anything is too small to list. For example, maybe one of the things that is wrong is a broken step on the back porch. Write it down. This is just another brain dump of the things you don't feel good about in your financial life that need to be corrected in some small or large way. Write it all down. Sometimes a poor idea leads you to great idea! We'll get to the solution

> *There are no financial problems, only spiritual ones.*

soon, for now let's just record what needs to be addressed.

When you complete this list, look your spouse in the eye and admit that for two really smart, good-looking people, you sure screwed up a lot, didn't you? Then laugh or cry, and let yourself feel the forgiveness of God. Submit it all to prayer. He's big enough to handle it.

What's missing in your finances and money? You're on your way to a better place and you're not going to let the cares of your world derail you. Now it's time to make a list of the gaps—things that need to be added to your life to make it better align with God's will for you. For example, maybe you need to protect Saturday nights and save some money so you and your spouse can have a date. Keep in mind as you create this list that the new direction you're taking is intended to take you closer to God—to align with His plan. So, as you reflect on what's missing, consider whether there are things you can add that will keep you focused on this new direction. For example, do you have a regular time set aside each day to talk to God and listen to Him speak to you

> *Spousal prayer is only a hand-holding distance away.*

through His word? Do you pray together? Even though Anne and I had been believers for some time, praying together was one of those things missing in our lives. When I suggested we try it, we both felt a little awkward about it. But I'll never forget that first time lying in bed in the dark, reaching for her hand, and saying a little prayer. We decided then and there that this was something we didn't want to miss anymore. And guys, I have to share something here. The first time I heard my wife pray and thank God for me, the "husband He had given her," it brought tears to my closed eyes. Spousal prayer is only a hand-holding distance away and one of our most powerful resources. Why don't you pause for few minutes right now and submit this list in prayer...together.

What's confusing about your finances and money? This may not be the longest of the four lists, but many times can be the most telling. With no ego or pride getting in the way, this question will let you say to each other, "I don't understand _____." It could be anything. "I don't understand our bank accounts. Why do I have to be the one in charge of all the finances? What's an IRA? What's the interest on our credit cards? I don't understand why we seem to have so many late charges. Why can't we go on vacations like our friends?"

> *Deferring financial responsibilities to only one spouse becomes a ticking time bomb.*

With most couples I've met there is usually one spouse who has the most questions, and is the most engaged, in completing this *Financial 4HL* list. If I had to comment on a trend I would share that in most cases this is a wife. It's not that husbands are smarter. (Yes, you can quote me on that.) It's because men are often the ones who handle the family finances and make the drastic mistake of not fully sharing the details with their wives. And the wife often defers to her husband—both are complicit in a dangerous practice that creates a passive growing potential wedge in their relationship. This bears repeating again. Deferring financial responsibilities to only one spouse becomes a ticking time bomb.

As long as everything goes well, it may not be a problem. But as soon as something goes wrong, the wife feels isolated, left out. The husband, feeling he was helping by taking care of all of these details, can feel overly responsible, can be overly critical of himself, sometimes even resentful. But when he looks in the mirror he knows it was his choice not to lead more clearly in the sensitive area of finances. That's when the ever-patient enemy moves in and uses this wedge to create discord. The wife may sense she should have been more involved and assertive, but it just wasn't her thing. The husband may feel he "should have taken the time to include her more deeply in discussing the risks involved." Life's tough enough without problems like these. So it's vitally important that any confusion over finances be brought to the surface in this exercise. I have also seen situations that are the exact opposite of the spousal roles above. Regardless of whose hands are on the money, you need to remain holding hands together.

> *Regardless of whose hands are on the money, you just need to remain holding hands.*

In most situations, a couple can get through these exercises just fine, but if you run into problems or communication lines begins to get stressed, take a break and take some time to pray. This is new territory for many of you. It probably took you a while to get in the shape you are now, so it will probably take you at least that long to understand your options and get it corrected.

If you do get to a point where the conversation gets emotional, or someone gets defensive and progress stops, you can always talk to one of *The Seven*. Maybe your Pastor or some godly counsel could facilitate some of these conversations with you. In addition, some of you reading this may need Christian marital counseling to go to the depths you really need to go. If you feel you do, please don't wait. Don't remain isolated and alone. Talk to someone immediately for support and courage to explore this option if needed. If this is you, I am praying for you in advance.

Another idea is that maybe you could facilitate this conversation for some of your friends, and they can facilitate for you in return. Not only does this create transparency, but it also builds a deeper relationship with your friends. However, if this is not an option, bathe the process in prayer as you go through it and give it your best shot.

The *Financial 4HL* exercise is designed to get everything on the table. As I shared earlier, resist the temptation to stop and try to fix anything. The goal is to define reality so that you know where you are. It's really a matter of establishing the starting point for your journey to recapture your life. You want to FIND YOUR NOW and place it squarely in your new plan back to a life by God's design. You're on your way back to Eden.

FIND YOUR NOW
STEP #3: RENEW FILTER

Now we move to FIND YOUR NOW Step #3, the ReNew Filter, a process to take the most important responses from the *Financial SQ* and *Financial 4HL* begin to position them for action and success. First, take the *FSQ* and *F4HL* lists you have prepared and pray over these lists and ask for God to show you the critical areas needing attention in your life. All of the items are important, but a few are likely more critical, more of an opportunity, and naturally more urgent.

I want to ask you to pause now for a moment and think about what you have just compiled, what these lists represent. Written on the paper you are holding in your hands is all of your praise, your successes, your hopes, your dreams, new plans, past mistakes, current confusion, and painful gaps. Have you ever had this kind of spiritual inventory in one place? Meditate on what you are holding. Give it to God. He wants it. He can handle it.

Cast all your cares on Him because He cares for you.
—1 Peter 5:7

Now read through the lists and highlight the items that God is leading you to focus on. A great way to get started is to pray to identify the *must do* goals from your larger list. You will have many items on your *SQ* and *4HL* lists, but I often see eight to twelve MUST DO action items highlighted by families. This is just an observation, you may have more; you may have less, that's okay. As you narrow your lists, look for these kind of common characteristics. A *must do* goal. . .

- . . .is something you feel God is asking you to do now
- . . .will remove a barrier in your relationship with Christ, or your marriage, bringing you closer together in that relationship
- . . .will grow and deepen your relationship with Christ, each other, and your family
- . . .is both important and urgent
- . . .meets an immediate positive financial requirement or result

Some common *must do* examples are:

o   We need to grow our worship through our giving.
o   We will pray together over our family financial choices.
o   We want to reduce what we spend 'eating out' and use that money to accelerate getting out of debt.

It is a core objective that you and your spouse are in agreement with the items chosen and commit to working together on them until completed. Remember what we started out to build for you: clarity, unity, and the beautiful context this final *ReNew Filter* brings.

As you finish narrowing your lists to your *must do* action items, prayerfully choose only two or three to focus on for starters. I have found that most families can take action on only two to three items at any one time. For some families it may even be just one, while others might be really great multi-taskers. The number doesn't matter as much as the progress toward the renewal of these important financial areas in your life. Save the unused items on your *FSQ* and *F4HL* lists as you can revisit them in the future and take action on them as you are led.

Now take each urgent item by itself and complete the

following detail:

- *Name the GOAL you want to RENEW?* Keep your goal focused and simple. If you can measure it, you can track it.
- *When do you want your GOAL COMPLETED?* It always helps to have a deadline.
- *How will you GLORIFY GOD?* We are called to glorify God in all that we do, and this goal is no different. By determining God's glory through your actions, you will remain in the center of His will.
- *What does the BIBLE say?* These are spiritual issues you are working through. Use your Bible's index to find related scriptures and wisdom for your goals.
- *Why is the goal MEANINGFUL to you?* What are the spiritual, emotional, and tangible reasons this is important? What will it feel like when you succeed?
- *Do you need to STOP DOING anything to make room for this?* The results of old choices can take up room in your life. The more you can remove, the more room you create for new choices and results.
- *Will you need to KEEP DOING anything to support it?* Many of your past results are good. What strengths, good choices, resources, etc. should you build upon?
- *What TRAPS and BARRIERS might you encounter on your way?* It's easy to fall back into old patterns. What are the obvious areas, people, situations, etc. that you should avoid? Sometimes you may have to change your playmates, your playgrounds, and your toys.
- *How will you use THE SEVEN to support you?* You need wisdom that will journey with you, encourage you, pray with you, and help you stay on track
- *What is your FIRST STEP toward your goal?* Any journey starts with one step. Make it simple, doable, and make it soon!

- ***What is your NEXT STEP toward your goal?*** If you always have a next step, you will keep moving toward your goal.

Once you start turning these lists into *ReNew* action items, you'll increasingly gain confidence that the life you wish you had is within your reach.

The results of FIND YOUR NOW are where you are now, and closer to Christ is where you're headed. One celebration at a time. One correction at a time. One addition at a time. One clarification at a time. You may already be feeling what lies ahead on your journey. God's word and wisdom, that once sat closed on a table, is being opened and relished each day. You look forward to your quiet moments together in prayer. They are becoming more meaningful and rich and you want them to last even longer.

One by one, you are removing the bricks from any barriers and throwing them away for good. The traps, once unobserved, once hidden, are now in plain view and being avoided. With diligence and intent, you are preparing for the hazards of life as best you can and you stand with your feet firmly planted with God at your side. The haze is lifting and you now know these financial issues you have been facing were not about the money, they were about your heart. You're putting it behind you and thinking about what God has for you today. You're living in your NOW.

LIVING FOR FREE

It took us all a while to get to where we are now. It will likely take you a while longer to get where God wants to take you. Some of you may have had too much fun with your credit card and that's what put you in this financial position. So what do you need to do after you have a party? It's time to clean up the mess.

But some of you didn't get into your financial trouble with a party; you were in a storm, often not of your own doing, and I'm sorry you've faced that. But after you catch you breath, what do you do after the storm has passed? Once again, as difficult as it may be, we have to pick up the pieces and clean up. Whether you created your mess or it was created for you, a cleanup needs to get underway. Pray for courage, insight, and focus as you begin. God will be with you every step of the way and He promises that the same spirit in his son Jesus Christ, he gives to everyone who follows Him.

Be strong and courageous. Do not be afraid or terrified because of them, for the LORD your God goes with you; he will never leave you nor forsake you.
—Deuteronomy 31:6

When you stumble—and you will, just as we have, and still do—turn to Scripture. Remember, God's word is true, reliable, and trustworthy. His plan far surpasses your own, and if you stay with it, you'll regain the joy and freedom that you once enjoyed in your little Eden.

This process of discovering where you are so you can determine where you need to go reminds me of the current popularity of old vinyl. Music fans are once again getting their audio on vinyl and turntables are being found and dusted off from parent's attics. These vinyl records began as a ball of hot plastic and went through a process of having grooves pressed into it that, when run over by the needle of a turntable, produce sound. Like the records of old, our years of wanting more, taking control, and getting what we asked for engraved our lives with grooves that produce the music in our lives that now are likely to feel out of tune. The only way to change our music, like that vinyl disc, is to melt it down, and re-press it with new grooves, and that's what you're doing. In order to melt something, you need heat. If you're feeling the heat from your efforts to recapture your life, use it to your advantage to melt

> *Let God use this heat to refine you and your dreams.*

away the old grooves. Let God use this heat to refine you and your dreams. You're getting closer to God's plan for you.

The most likely source of heat will come in the form of tension and disagreements because if you and your spouse are doing this right, you're going to strike some nerves in each other. It's one thing to agree that you need to create a family budget. It's quite another to say, "Honey, in order to cut down our transportation expenses, we've got to sell the car and buy something less expensive. The insurance alone on that vehicle is killing us." But you love that car, and instead of accepting this wisdom from your very thoughtful spouse, you start thinking of all the things your spouse spends money on that *they* could change. I think you know the heat I'm talking about.

> The enemy is at his best when he is keeping you isolated, keeping you prideful, keeping you distracted, and keeping you afraid.

This heat is good. But, heat is still uncomfortable. When the temperature climbs, most people head for the shade, but you don't have to because you're not alone. This may be a time when you call in one of *The Seven*. Maybe a trusted couple or a more experienced, godly man or woman could join you to keep the temperature manageable. This is definitely a time for prayer. Sometimes we talk so glibly about the church as the body of Christ but never really let it function in our lives. It looks a lot like pride when we feel that way. We don't want anyone else to know we are having these financial problems. Again, the enemy is at his best when he is keeping you isolated, keeping you prideful, keeping you distracted, and keeping you afraid. Here's a great opportunity to let the Church be the Church.

There's another force that will attempt to derail you on your journey: regret and shame. You're going to have to address mistakes that you've made and that's never easy. I know. Within a few months after I bought our third house, I knew I had made a mistake. And when *I* say I bought our third house, that was the first mistake because I really did not consult with anyone, including my wife. We spoke about it, but I wanted it and I got what I wanted. That's always a recipe for disaster. When God revealed the poor decision I had made, I didn't have the courage to tell Anne until almost a year later. I'll never forget sitting on the floor of my study with her and, through some shared tears, discussed that while our house was a good investment, I felt God was leading us to sell our house and downsize. Don't get me wrong, we could have afforded to stay, at least for a while, but I could feel that it would be a barrier to God's plans even though I had no clue what His plans were going to be. To her credit, once again, after a few weeks of trying to process what I had shared with her, I came home from work one day and she was all smiles.

"I went online today, and guess what? I found a lot of houses that I think would be just right for us."

Every man should have such a godly woman; and I should have been thrilled, but I wasn't. The ever-patient enemy always waits for the most opportune time, and he knew that I felt bad about my mistake. And I listened to his whisper: "You give people financial advice, but you don't even follow it yourself." Goodness, that hurt! But it was this pain that drove me to make some of the changes in my life that I'm recommending here. I soon surrounded myself with godly people I could go to with any financial decision. I made the commitment to involve Anne early and often rather than trying to go it alone. Finances are not really her thing, but she is trying and it's getting better every single month as I see her feeling more involved and in tune with our plans. Perhaps most important, I began to trust and apply God's word to my money matters. True financial freedom for me was freedom from my money, regardless of my money.

The whispers will continue. The enemy will never give up. But by using *The Seven* you will increasingly recognize his lies. The enemy desires to steal all you have, and put a wedge between you and God any time, anywhere, anyhow. The enemy wants it all.

We started this journey in our own little Eden. Then something happened. In his epic poem, *Paradise Lost*, John Milton recreates the biblical account of the temptation of Adam and Eve and their expulsion from the Garden of Eden. An acquaintance of Milton's read the poem—some 10,000 lines long—and asked the poet, "Thou has said much here of Paradise Lost, but what hast thou to say of Paradise Found?" So the poet sat down and wrote *Paradise Regained*, which chronicled the account of Jesus being tempted in the wilderness by Satan. I'm the last guy to analyze poetry, but I find it interesting that regaining

> *The enemy wants it all.*

paradise, according to Milton, only happens through Jesus. His triumph over evil gives you and me the hope for something better than we currently experience. Jesus obeyed His father, came to earth, and carried our sins to the cross so we can start over. We may not be able to return to the garden just yet, but we can enjoy the life God intended for us by placing our complete trust in Him on our journey. That's living for God. That's living for free.

I have thought of that building map in China many times. That funny phrase on the map reminds me that God only promises today, this moment, this NOW. God is taking us places, destinations to be determined. Futures are waiting to unfold. Yet we are to focus on each day only as it comes, seeking Him alone, and bringing Him glory. We are to be wise stewards, expecting Him to show up in the midst of our everyday lives, just as He showed up the day He found you and you found Him. You are exactly where He wants you to be right at this moment. He has plans for you this day—a journey yet to unfold. It's the ultimate do-over, or what the theologians call redemption.

REFLECTION

CHANGE FOR YOUR DOLLAR

1) Just as you would not start a trip without knowing where

you are and where you want to go, you can't build a strong and thriving financial future if you don't have a sense of your foundation and your destination.

2) It's important to spend time together to reflect, to plan and to pray on your trek to find clarity, unity and context.

3) Every journey includes hazards and traps. The key is to get yourself back on the path as soon as you realize you're off course.

4) There is nothing useful in consistently looking behind you, or trying to see too far into the future. Keep your eyes focused on the now directly in front of you.

MONEY IN MOTION

1) Consider how many productive years you believe you have left and what God would have you do with that time.

2) If you and your spouse are not on God's plan take a look at where are you going and the plan you have to get there. If you don't have a plan, sit with your spouse and begin developing one.

3) Name one financial choice that will immediately jumpstart your journey and bring you closer to God's will for your life (hint...think generosity).

4) I recommend we should always remember to start any planning process with celebration and praise. Think of ways you can incorporate that into your life.

5) Share a tune from your own old vinyl that needs to be melted down and re-grooved. Think of some old lie that still plays in your mind today and takes you away from God.

PRAYER

I'm working so hard but I don't seem to be getting anywhere. I can't keep up with the world. It's moving too fast. I'm afraid sometimes that if I slow down, I'll get swept away. Maybe that's exactly what

I need to do—to stop chasing after the world and let myself get swept away by you. You promise to catch me. You promise to be there. You promise me life that is truly life. Let me know your plan for my life, Lord. Guide me to discover it. Help me live now, in this moment, following you and you alone. Lord, hear my prayer. Amen.

starting together...again

Therefore, if anyone is in Christ, the new creation has come:
The old has gone, the new is here!
We are therefore Christ's ambassadors,
as though God were making his appeal through us.
We implore you on Christ's behalf: Be reconciled to God.
God made Him who had no sin to be sin for us,
so that in Him we might become the righteousness of God.
—2 Corinthians 5:17, 20-21

I like bologna, but not every week. I like patio furniture, but not in the kitchen. McDonald's? If we have to. Our little garden of Eden was nice when we were just starting out, but I really wouldn't want to go back, even if we could. But we can't. Like Adam and Eve, we left the garden when we took a bite out of that delicious looking lie: "God doesn't really mean what he says, does he? He's holding out on you. You deserve everything you want and will be happier when you get it."

That innocence we enjoyed can never be fully reclaimed. The steps you have begun to take will reward you with the joy that God has always wanted for you and a peace that emanates from His spirit deep within you.

PROGRESS, NOT PERFECTION

It won't happen overnight, and there will be bumps along the way. Physically, financially, and materially—you will likely build more barriers, more traps will await, and you will encounter more hazards in your path. When you slip, get up, brush yourself off, and keep moving forward. Emotionally and spiritually you can get back on track in an instant—it's merely a choice. Poor choices will happen again—the enemy will continue looking for the most opportune time to remind you the apple is still there, juicy, delicious, and temporarily satisfying. He will whisper: "See, it will never work. It's just too demanding. And look at all you're missing. You don't see your neighbor moving to a smaller house, do you?" It bears repeating: If you let it, comparison destroys contentment, and then creates it.

Remember, the goal here is progress, not perfection—moving toward a life that looks like God's plan and less like your own. Less of me, more of God. Or as John writes: *"He must become greater; I must become less"* (John 3:30). It's about wanting more of God than what the world offers. You will find that your perception of your money issues will also begin to diminish when you think less about money and more about God. Each day you live in God's provision rather than your own, you will gain more strength to do it again the next day. And the next. And the next. You're living for free.

With all my efforts to look successful, you know what it got me? Exhaustion. I was like the guy at the magic show trying to keep all the plates spinning. He started out easily enough—putting one plate on top of a dowel, giving it a spin, and going on to the next. Each time he added a plate it got a little harder. And then after he got the third plate going, the first one began to slow down and start wobbling, so he had to rush back to that one and give it another spin, and then hustle to add a fourth plate to the mix. That was me. Make a little money, get a bigger or better something, which meant I had to make a little more. Catch the plate just before it

> *God's plan was always intended to give me a life rather than a lifestyle.*

drops. Get it spinning again. Repeat. All I was doing was sprinting to stay in some crazy race I would never win.

A friend recently asked me how my life changed after I abdicated the throne in my little "k" kingdom. I think he wanted to hear that all of our financial issues had been solved and

> *Think destination before you think direction.*

we were living happily ever after. My answer was a little more realistic and honest: the biggest change in my life was relief! I don't have to keep up with anyone, including myself, or anything else, except God's plan. God's plan was always intended to give me a life rather than a lifestyle. He wants me to live for free.

You will find that this new journey you've begun can also be exhilarating and energizing. As you free yourself from the burden of keeping up, you'll wonder whatever possessed you to try so hard to build your own little "k" kingdom in the first place. Instead of trying to please so many people, I now only have to please an audience of One: God. And trust me, pleasing God is a whole lot easier than trying to live up to some unrealistic image imposed on us by a culture that says you only matter if you look like this, live here, or own that. It's incredible how the applause of One can sound so sweet and drown out so much.

Progress will feel lighter and fresher. By consciously choosing to discard the stuff and activities that tie us to this world, we're going to make more room for God to operate in our lives. We're creating an openness to His perfect plans for us—creating margin so we can serve Him by serving others. Your wish list will change from bigger, better, faster to lighter, fresher, nimbler. We're living for free.

We're taking control again, but in a different way—instead of having it our way and getting what we think we want, we're giving the wheel back to God. It's fascinating that we take control by releasing control. With every money decision, we're moving toward God, not away from Him. Think destination before you think direction. You'll get there, but enjoy the ride today, this moment. Savor your newfound freedom from the unrelenting pressure to borrow, buy, and build.

Do Anne and I still have disagreements over money? Yes, but not as many and without the stress-induced frustration and harshness. Plus, because we're now on the same page, the solutions to those problems come easier. Are we still tempted to buy something we don't need? Of course. And sometimes we can't resist. Do you think there's a reason that company calls itself Apple?!

One of my favorite children's stories is the Aesop fable, "City Mouse, Country Mouse." As you probably recall, a mouse that lived in the city invited his cousin to visit from his humble and sparse country home. But whenever they sat down to the sumptuous feast the city mouse provided, they were always interrupted by the dogs and cats in the mansion and could not fully enjoy the bounty offered on the sumptuous table for they were running for their lives. After he could take it no longer, the country mouse and his mouse bride returned to their simpler life in the country. The moral of this fable: A modest life with peace and quiet is better than a rich one with danger and strife. Like the country mouse so eloquently shared, "I prefer to eat simple food in peace."

PACKING LIGHT

There isn't a formula to figure out how much money you need, or can handle, to live life and still honor God, but this prayer, which I have adapted from a wonderful nugget of wisdom in Proverbs, helps me keep money in perspective: "Lord don't give me so much that I forget about you or so little that I do things that would not honor you. Just give me enough so I stay close to you" (see Proverbs 30:8-9). How different from the prayers most of us have prayed at one time or another: "Lord, please help me get that raise, or get that deal, or make that sale, so I don't have to worry so much about money." Be honest. Has more money ever ended your worries about money?

I'm also often asked questions like, "But doesn't God want me to enjoy my money? I mean, He gave me a good job; I work hard, and I am now able to afford nicer things. What's wrong with that?" We have to be very careful how we answer that question because our tendency has often been to rationalize our love of money by saying—and truthfully so—that it all comes from God. So I always answer by reminding people that God doesn't necessarily want you rich or poor, but content in only Him and honoring Him with your life, and that includes your financial choices, what you wear, where you live, what you drive, and how you give, which means you need to stay focused on *His* plans, not yours. Remember, you are on *His* journey.

Of course this new journey you've taken offers more than relief. It positions you better to love God and serve others, which is the ultimate source of joy and fulfillment. Many—if not most—Christian couples truly want to do something significant for the Kingdom, but usually decide to put it off until they can afford the time and money. They'd love to take their entire family on a mission trip, but they're maxed out and too busy to try to raise funds. Or they'd like to negotiate a new work arrangement to free up some time to mentor teenagers or volunteer with a non-profit, but how will they live off the reduced income? We want the abundant life that comes from serving God and others, but the lifestyle that we have built may not let us have it. Some of the tallest barriers to God have been built by us.

One time, we were headed out for a vacation, and as we were leaving I could hardly see to back out of the driveway because our SUV was stuffed to the ceiling with stuff we hoped to enjoy when we got to our destination: suitcases with way more clothes than any of us would wear, duffel bags with games and sporting equipment to keep us busy (who wants to be busy on a vacation?), coolers, folding chairs, pillows. You'd think we were moving to a new house, not heading to the beach for a week. We always enjoyed our vacations, but it seemed like half the time I was either packing or unpacking all the stuff we brought along.

Like loading up an SUV for a trip, I think most of us tend to pack heavy for our everyday life journey. Except the suitcases are houses, the bags are cars, the sports equipment are expensive toys and belongings, the beach chairs are investments and money, and the coolers full of food are all of the luxuries we enjoy. I have so much stuff packed around me that it's almost impossible for me to get a clear view of where I am going. I've created piles of stuff blocking my view of God's plans for me. Forget being in a position to execute those plans. As a counselor once told my father-in-law who was working diligently to make a major life change occur, "Sometimes you have to change your playground and your playmates." (And I think many of us may have to swap out our toys as well!)

FREEDOM TO FOLLOW

Can you imagine what it would feel like being free enough to have the option to take off whenever you sensed God leading you into a new adventure—to be able to drop what you were doing and just go?

A number of years ago, I had the rare privilege of hearing Joe Stowell, current President of Cornerstone University, speak to our Charlotte Leadership Forum small group. His message was simple and centered on Matthew 4:19-20. This is the time when Jesus stopped by the fishermen and said two words, "Follow me." The scripture says, "At once they left their nets and followed him." Joe's question to us at the end of his address was simple, too. "What nets are you holding that you need to release to follow God?" The nets of these fisherman represented their identity and their livelihood. It was what they trusted to make their life work. Jesus was asking them to drop them. To let them go along with all they represented then follow Jesus. He's offering us the same invitation today. Will *you* follow Him?

When the disciples were sent out to spread the gospel they

were given a very *specific* set of packing instructions.

> *And he sent them out to proclaim the kingdom of God and to heal the sick. He told them: "Take nothing for the journey—no staff, no bag, no bread, no money, no extra shirt. Whatever house you enter, stay there until you leave that town. If people do not welcome you, leave their town and shake the dust off your feet as a testimony against them"*
>
> —Luke 9:2-5

You may ask, "Why these instructions?" So they would depend solely on God as they carried out His mission. They would have little to take care of—little to distract them—leaving them free to serve those in their path and trust their provision to God's generous hands. They were packing for *One*. When you look more like the disciples, your stuff does not become a drain on resources and there is less time devoted to caring for it. You can make adjustments quickly, you have more freedom from your finances, and less distraction for the plans God has in

Move from fat and happy to thin and joyful.

store. I'm not there yet, but I hope to get to the point where I can say to Anne, "Let's go!" With little packing, few worries about our stuff, and just enough financial reserves to fund our God-inspired adventure. That's living for free.

I like thinking that we're making a move from fat and happy to thin and joyful. Happiness is a fleeting emotion based on circumstances; joy is a companion that remains constant no matter how much or how little you have. To be honest, fat and happy is easier, and that's because we allowed ourselves to be externally motivated. We just went with the flow of our friends, neighbors, and colleagues who believed that if we just had more, life would be better. To reap the benefits of thin and joyful, you have work out, and getting in shape is never easy.

I don't know about you, but working out doesn't come naturally for me. I want to be internally motivated—possessing a desire from inside that will get me off the couch and into something active, but it's difficult. I need someone to workout with me, to hold me accountable. I also try to imagine how much better I will look if I stick with it. My body is the temple of God, albeit God's temple is a little soft around the edges these days! So when you're tempted to roll over on your back and float downstream with everyone else, it's time to start swimming . . . upstream, against the flow, stroke-by-stroke as you watch everyone else lazily letting the current carry them along. Make no mistake; the resistance you face will be daunting. Your friends might think you're crazy. Your neighbors won't understand why you're "moving backward." You'll even have those moments when you wonder if you're doing the right thing.

Continually remind yourself that you're not just working on your finances or trying to manage your money better. You're getting your life back. You're turning *from* what will eventually rust, break, or get stolen (see Matthew 6:19) and turning *toward* what will last; what delivers more than you could ever hope (see Matthew 6:33). It's living for free.

So how do you know if you're headed in the right direction? As with any journey to new destination, it always makes good sense to set a few checkpoints along the way to give you visual and mental confirmation you are moving in a positive direction. (It's the Eagle Scout coming out in me—always be prepared.) The best ones I know of are a set of questions based on memories of those early days when things were simpler. Periodically ask yourselves:

- Am I desiring more of God?
- Is this feeling like a special time in my life or just the same old same old?
- Is my life becoming any simpler, less cluttered?
- Do I feel closer to my spouse?

- Are my daily spiritual disciplines more consistent?
- Do I seem more like "the old me?"
- Can I point to a specific experience of serving or helping someone?
- Am I loving my neighbors?
- Can I talk about money issues without getting upset or defensive?
- Am I more patient?
- Am I becoming more forgiving?
- Am I growing in generosity and giving?
- Do I have—and take—opportunities to do things spontaneously?
- Do I have a few close friends and am I spending enjoyable time with them?
- When I need something am I ever likely to borrow it?
- Am I more concerned about my relationship with God than with building our wealth?

Don't expect a yes to every one of these questions at the outset of—or even months into—your new journey. In fact, it may take several weeks before you get your first yes. But each time you pull this list out and go over it together, you could be able to add one or two more answers into the 'yes' column. As that happens, you can be confident that you're on your way to something better than where you've been. That would also be a good excuse to celebrate! Sometimes just holding hands as you walk to get ice cream can work wonders!

God in his great unwavering mercy invites us to start over. Together. With Him. Again. And again, if necessary. Every moment, every morning (see Lamentations 3:22-23). Those early years that we remember so fondly? He offers something far better than bologna sandwiches and unmatched furniture. He offers Himself and the adventure of trusting Him completely. Because I now crave the joy God has for me, I'm learning to live with less world and more God. I'm learning to live for free.

We're all familiar with the stark warning from Jesus: *"No one can serve two masters. Either you will hate the one and love the other, or you will be devoted to the one and despise the other. You cannot serve both God and money"* (Matthew 6:24).

Ron Blue helped me understand that the actual word that Jesus used was *doulos*, translated as *slave*. Let's insert the translation into the scripture and read it the way it was intended: *"No one can serve two masters. Either you will hate the one and love the other, or you will be devoted to the one and despise the other. You cannot be a slave to both God and money"* (Matthew 6:24).

You can't be a slave to both God and money—you have to choose, but you will still be a slave to one or the other. Slavery implies ownership, and this really is the heart of the issue. You're either going to be owned by money and the world, or you're going to be owned by God. Most of us have tried to have both. As I shared earlier in the book, you can have God and you can have money, but you **cannot** love them both. God tells us we have to choose. The turmoil and discomfort we experience in our finances is a direct result of not choosing. Money will never be enough, nor can we ever have enough, thus leaving us in a constant state of wanting more but never getting it. That is, until we choose to be a slave to Christ.

Singer/songwriter Bob Dylan echoed Matthew 6, when he wrote, the song, "Gotta Serve Somebody."

"You're gonna have to serve somebody/It may be the devil or it may be the Lord/But you're gonna have to serve somebody."

Eve heard the whisper of the enemy and chose to listen. Adam chose poorly when he listened to Eve. God came to find them and they were hiding. It's hard to make excuses with a mouth full of apple.

Most Christian families make money decisions with little or no understanding of the forces that impact those decisions. They may hear the whisper, or they may choose poorly. Either way, they are not free. I prayed to be transparent as I shared the deeper choices, questions, mysteries, and opportunities I believe we each need to confront before God. He asks that we follow Him and His plan, not ours—to put Him ahead of everything else in our lives. As we do that, money ceases to be a distraction. Whether we are given a lot or a little, it will be enough.

Our financial choices are a window into who we are, what we believe, and who or what we trust. You've probably figured it out by now. That's really what this book is all about—we equate money with freedom, but we're designed to equate freedom with God. As you journey toward this redefined financial freedom, my prayer for you now is that you will determine whom you will serve. It is all His gifts, His plan, and your choice.

Once you choose God, and God alone, whether abundance or scarcity may come, you will rest in that sweet and peaceful place where God is your only desire and money is only another resource used to honor Him as you live for free.

REFLECTION

CHANGE FOR YOUR DOLLAR

1) You will not get it right every time, but your focus should not be perfection. It should be progress toward what God wants for you.
2) If you are still so burdened by possessions and the responsibility of tending to them that you aren't free to follow God, you may have some unpacking to do.
3) Having your checkpoints clearly defined allows you to confirm at any time that you are on the right track.
4) It's time to choose a master. Will you be a slave to stuff or a faithful servant of God? Choose wisely.

MONEY IN MOTION

1) If you have ever thought about downsizing in any areas of your life, think about the appeal and the concerns that arise from that task.
2) Taking a prayerfully educated guess at His plans for you, write down where He might be leading you.
3) If time or money were not an issue, name three things that you would love to do today that would fall under the category of loving God or loving others.
4) Name one financial choice that is coming up soon and try to identify what God's plan is for it. Identify the resources it affects and how you will choose to proceed.

PRAYER

Lord you are the beginning and the end. How I want to rely on your truths! Thank you for the hope and confidence you give us to know you and worship you. You allow us to make our own choices but you never stop loving us. You let us travel our own paths, knowing sometimes that they are taking us further from you, yet you faithfully wait for us. Forgive us for the times where we took advantage of your love and forgiveness. Will you let us start together with you yet one more time? Will you free us of any distractions between us? Give us your wisdom and the courage to follow you. Will you take us toward the garden once again? Amen.

thanks to so many...

- I found treasure in Ethiopia with Steve, Flint, Casey & Joe.
- A dinner with Steve, Janet, Flint, Julie, Casey, Wesley, Joe & Kay where I shared that "I believe God wants me to write a book," and we prayed.
- An inspired cup of coffee with Wesley & Wendy, who introduced me to a friend.
- I learned to *compel* and so much more with Lysa, Renee, Lindsey, Amy, Barb, & team.
- Laurie, who kept things quiet at work, so I could write on my days away.
- Rennie, Debby, Terry, Jamie, Ken, Steady & Randy—our NCFP board who encourages me to follow a journey led by an amazing God.
- A new friend named Esther who liked my ideas—and her team, Lauren, Whitney, Jessica, Lisa, Brigette and Jackie who are guiding me so well.
- Karen started from scratch with me and taught me how to gather my thoughts.
- Cara who made sure what I wrote, looked and sounded like English.
- Bruce helped me get my words together and taught me how to speak them well.
- Whitney captured the light and saved the day...and didn't even use a D-40.
- My buddy Mike, who introduced me to Bob, where I learned to think big.
- "Big brother" Lloyd who introduced me to Lyn.
- Lyn, a man of God and a gifted sage who ordered and shaped my writing . . . and who still needs to catch one more fish to tie me.
- My other friend Bob, who taught me about mastery of life

at the feet of our Lord.

- Rennie, Casey and Chip made it possible for me to write in lovely, tranquil places.
- The other JP, who liked the way I told stories and I found myself on radio.
- Gary, my friend and radio guru and Josh who made me sound like a pro.
- David & Jason, who are as inspiring as they are fun.
- Alex & Stephen, I learned more about prayer by watching and listening to you.
- Steve & Janet, Jay & Olga, and Flint & Julie were answers to prayer.
- For the guidance of my godly counsel and prayer partner Percy.
- Ron, the money master, who taught me what the Bible says about money.
- Ken, who challenged me to think of my practice as a ministry.
- Mike, a pastor who changed the trajectory of my life.
- The Barney boys, Chip, Patrick, Harry & Joe who have been laughing with me, encouraging me, helping me and praying for me for a long time.
- Mom & Dad, who taught me on the farm to work hard, be polite & love the Lord.
- Four big brothers, Bill, Walter, Bobby & Harry – thanks for not killing me!
- Three fun and funny kids - Jay, Lynn & Haley whom I love with all my heart and I know they are cheering for their Dad – you are a gift to me and your mom.
- . . . and the best for last, my beautiful, sweet wife Anne, for her love, support and unwavering belief in me long before I saw it in myself.

endnotes

1. Northwestern Mutual – How Our Financial Misbehaviors Turn into Money Maladies (REV12/05)

2. John W. Kennedy, "The Debt Slayers," Christianity Today, May 2006, http://www.christianitytoday.com/ct/2006/may/23.40.html

3. R. Leigh Coleman, "Credit Card Debt and Financial Woes in America," Christian Post, July 2011, http://www.christianpost.com/news/plastic-debt-at-an-all-time-high-52056/

4. Katherine T. Phan, "New Year Bring New Hope for Bible Literacy" Christian Post, December 2010, http://www.christianpost.com/news/new-year-new-hope-for-turning-the-tide-of-Bible-illiteracy-48279/

5. Louise Stoy, "Anywhere the Eye Can See, It's Likely to See an Ad," The New York Times, January 2011, http://www.nytimes.com/2007/01/15/business/media/15everywhere.html?_r=0

6. "Do prospects trust you enough to answer this one question?," Strategic Coach, http://blog.strategiccoach.com/dan-sullivans-r-factor-question/